DIVINE DAILY PRESCRIPTIONS

OLAYINKA DADA, M.D.

authorHOUSE°

AuthorHouse™
1663 Liberty Drive
Bloomington, IN 47403
www.authorhouse.com
Phone: 833-262-8899

Published by AuthorHouse 08/06/2020

ISBN: 978-1-7283-6706-4 (sc)
ISBN: 978-1-7283-6705-7 (e)

Library of Congress Control Number: 2020912998

Print information available on the last page.

DEDICATION

To my daughter, Mary-Favour Adeoluwa Dada. I appreciate your heart of worship and desire to follow in the footsteps of your father. May the Lord grant you all the desires of your heart. May you be blessed forever.

ACKNOWLEDGEMENTS

Thanks be to God for His mercies and blessings. I am deeply indebted to God.

I also appreciate my spiritual parents, daddy and mommy Adeboye, for their love, exemplary faith and impartation.

My appreciation also goes to my family members and the Restoration House Hamilton family, for their love and understanding.

My deepest appreciation to my wife, Oluwatoyin, for her values, love, sacrifices and devotion. I also appreciate deeply our children—Timothy, Esther, Mary-Favour and Deborah-Peace—for their understanding and love.

DAY

1

COURAGE

TEXT: PSALM 27:14 NKJV

"Wait on the Lord; Be of good courage, And He shall strengthen your heart; Wait, I say, on the Lord!"

KEY NUGGET: **Be the courageous person the world needs because God's love melts fears!**

An African adage says, *"When a child gets to a fearful place, he will be scared."* In the same way, fear rules over those who are kids spiritually and toddlers emotionally too. However, courage is needed to deal with fear because it is the ability to have control over fear in tough and difficult situations. It could be defined as bravery, grit, dare and boldness. Courage is not the absence of fear; rather, courage is the mastery of fear.

Our text is explicit on the foundation for building courage and that is: waiting on the Lord! Waiters in restaurants build courage on what to serve by listening to clients place their orders. The confidence to serve comes from what the customer says to them. Our courage only becomes strong when we wait for God to speak to us and place an order so to speak. One of the floods that erode people's courage in life is impatience. Courage doesn't just jump on anyone; it is built through waiting. A man who bows to God in waiting cannot be bent by the intimidation of men.

The heart is the seat of courage; the strength of the heart determines the weight of courage it can carry. A man can look hard and tough with an intimidating stature on the outside, but this doesn't necessarily translate to a strong heart. Whereas another man may look fragile and slim, yet carry a very strong heart, because he has waited on the Lord. The primary place to find evidence of a man who has received strength from the Lord to confront his challenges is the heart. How easily does your heart pound in fear? What gets your heart soaked in fear?

A teenage girl grew up scared of cockroaches. While having dinner one night, a cockroach flew across the dining table and landed close to food. As she hastened in a frightened response to move her plate away from the cockroach, she ended up spilling the whole food. Though the cockroach never touched her, her fearful reaction led to the loss of her costly meal. Yes, she was bigger than the roach and had the resources to eliminate the threat, but her heart was too weak to confront the situation. There are people today who have wasted their life's opportunities and privileges because of fear and the lack of courage to take the bull by the horns. Where there is no courage to confront issues, an ant would often look like a giant. Many have lost courage due to childhood fears, some due to misinformation and taboos while others are due to the environments and experiences that influenced their biological development.

Lack of courage tends to rob people of their rights and inheritances. It robbed Saul of his relevance as the king of Israel when he was confronted by Goliath. However, it was the courage to confront this same Goliath that brought David into the limelight (see 1 Samuel 17 KJV). It is not the size of the dog in a fight that determines the victory; it is the size of the fight in the dog.

I often wonder why God repeated Himself thrice when charging Joshua to take over the mantle from Moses. In Joshua chapter 1, verses 6, 7 and 9 KJV, God admonished Joshua to, *"Be strong and of good courage."* Even though God had promised Joshua His ever-abiding presence, Joshua was still aware of the need to be strong and of good courage.

It should be emphasized here that the kind of courage Joshua was enjoined to have was well qualified as "good courage". This would imply that people can have bad courage to commit heinous crimes. Some are timid when it comes to telling the truth but possess the courage to lie and defraud others. There are women who lack the courage to confront inappropriate practices in their workplaces but have the courage to disrespect their husbands at home and dishonor the Lord. Some young men lack the good courage to turn down the evil advances of their peers but can easily muster enough bad courage to disregard the godly instructions of their parents.

In my leadership life, I have come to discover that many people lack good courage. Some people would rather grumble, complain, and engage in backtalk than confront their problems due to their many-sided fears. Today's world is full of people-pleasers around who are afraid to stand up for what is right.

Courage is very essential to godly living in an ungodly world. Courage is needed in order to:

- Be a voice that speaks out the truth amid errors
- Hold on to the truth of God in the pool of falsehood
- Stand your ground in the face of many threats.
- Launch into the deep when you are not sure of the outcome.
- Be a light in this dark world.

Please God and do His perfect will in this sinful and perverse world.

You can grow in courage by waiting on the Lord to hear His Word by praying, fasting, going and growing through the process necessary for the promise and having fellowship with godly and bold people. In addition, confront your fears and believe God to strengthen your heart. His love overwhelms and surrounds you, washing your sins and fears away.

This world needs courageous men and women and I am persuaded you can be one of them.

PRAYER SHOTS:

1. I will be courageous. I will not be afraid, alarmed or terrified.
2. I pray for new strength in my innermost being.
3. I won't catch the air of fear in my world; Lord, separate me from the virus of fear circulating in our society- social network, cable news, negative people.

DAY

THERE ARE LESSONS IN
ALL SEASONS OF LIFE

TEXT: 1 PETER 4:12 NKJV

"Beloved, do not think it strange concerning the fiery trial which is to try you, as though some strange thing happened to you."

KEY NUGGET: Don't be bewildered when life gets difficult. Rejoice, because you are suffering for God's glory and you are about to graduate to the next level!

Most times we miss God's blessings because we fail the lessons of trials. A friend shared his growing up story under parents who were both tough disciplinarians. At a point in his teenage years, he concluded that his parents were wicked, so he sought ways to escape from their grip but without success. It was after he grew up that he realized that the seeds of their tough principles and instructions had blossomed in him into a tree of responsibility and hard work. Now, he sees these same parents as heroes.

Our perceptions are usually the first challenge of the fiery trials we face. They seem strange to our thoughts and alien to God's promises. They are usually strange to our expectations and petitions to God. Peter was quick to address our perception of trials because we cannot perform better than our perception of such. We should mature to the point of familiarity with fiery trials, which God often employs to furnish us to His taste. From the onset, Joseph's trials looked strange in comparison to his dreams, but they were ordained routes to God's intention for him. While his brothers thought they were selling him, they didn't realize they were sending him to his place of making. He arrived as a slave into a land he would eventually rule. The trust he would earn in the future required the qualification and certification of trials. God only trusts those he duly tries.

Nothing restricts the growth of capacity in a man more than his comfort. We cannot extend our influence over God's intended destination while settled in our place of ease. Until we are stretched; we cannot spread into maximum possibilities. God knows our breaking point. He will not try us beyond what we can handle and bear. It is not strange when a man of promise sojourns in his prophetic land like a stranger; it is called process. Every product reflects its process; and, the better the process the more durable the product. What you cannot withstand, you cannot witness or introduce to others.

We must not allow fiery trials to manipulate our thoughts and twist our perception. The closest border to the day is the darkest of the night. Weeping might last for a night, but joy comes in the morning (see Psalm 30:5 NKJV).

God knows how to hide the miraculous in the ridiculous. We only need to cooperate with Him in thought and actions. He would not allow what we cannot handle to happen to us. It is often said that life is not a bed of roses, but what we need to realize, however, is that roses are plucked from thorny trees despite their beauty. Adversity tends to reflect our strength. Proverbs 24:10 says KJV, "If thou faint in the day of adversity, thy strength is small." We often assume we have capacity for the blessing until God allows the weight of trials to be thrown at us. If trials can break you, then it's more likely the blessings can crush you too.

Growth takes place as we exercise our muscles, joints and organs. The trials, tragedies and difficulties we pass through are meant to make us stronger and better. In other words, they are designed for our good and not to make us bitter. We should, therefore, allow them to accomplish their purposes and seek to learn every possible lesson they come with. I must confess that it took me and my wife some time to understand the truth behind trials. We were able to discover that if we don't handle the trials or tests well, we might be stuck in a perpetual cycle of dealing with the same trials again and again for much longer than necessary. Today, we first give thanks to God in every trial that confronts us, we then pray for him to give us the power to overcome them and carefully identify lessons to be learnt.

The "Nevers" of trials:

- Never quit
- Never curse God
- Never complain
- Never get angry
- Never be bitter
- Never be sad
- Never be self-righteous.

If you handle every trial well, you will advance in your walk towards destiny.

PRAYER SHOTS:

1. Lord, please release the grace to finish strong and well on me.
2. Grant me the wisdom, strength and stability to fulfil my life's destined projects.
3. Help me not to quit or abandon my dreams and visions along the way.

DAY

RESIST THE DEVIL

TEXT: 1 PETER 5:8-9 NKJV

"BE SOBER; BE VIGILANT; BECAUSE YOUR ADVERSARY THE
DEVIL WALKS ABOUT LIKE A ROARING LION, SEEKING WHOM
HE MAY DEVOUR. RESIST HIM, STEADFAST IN THE FAITH,
KNOWING THAT THE SAME SUFFERINGS ARE EXPERIENCED
BY YOUR BROTHERHOOD IN THE WORLD."

KEY NUGGET: Be alert and take a decisive stand against the devil
or else he will advance by more than a yard!

The mentioning of Satan's name around some people makes them
quake in fear. They walk about trying to avoid the devil and his troubles.
This mindset has pushed many to publish books about the devil and raise
prayer ministries dedicated to "binding" the devil. It is laughable that
Christians could display such a level of ignorance by praying that the
devil—a spirit being—should die or be bound! These kinds of approaches
in confronting the devil have no scriptural base and thus ineffective in
defeating him.

The first attitude a Christian must have in overcoming the devil
is sobriety; being clearheaded and not drunk with self-confidence
or assumptions. Some Christians are defeated today because they are

intoxicated by their gifts, wealth or positions. They make bogus claims out of pride to impress people only for them to be stricken once by the devil and they're not able to recover. There's an African proverb that says, *"A man who is not armed with the drug for nausea should not eat what can irritate his guts."* No believer overcomes the devil's aggression simply by wishes, but by following scriptural prescriptions.

As believers in Christ Jesus, the Scriptures admonish us to be vigilant, observant, watchful and sensitive among many other instructions. Sadly, many saints have been victims of the devil simply because of their carelessness! Many ministers have become prey to the devil not for lack of anointing or gifting, but because of insensitivity and failure to pay attention to the devil's subtlety. You cannot live carelessly in life and still have victory over the devil.

It is obvious that God wants us to first focus on our becoming sober and vigilant before setting out to launch our campaign against the devil and his kingdom.

The devil is our adversary and nothing he does is to your advantage, no matter how juicy his offers. Eve believed that the serpent's offer in the garden was to her benefit until her eyes were opened to the truth, but it was too late. Whatever the benefits people get from carrying out devilish acts eventually ends up working against them.

Obviously, the devil is not static; he changes positions and tactics so you wouldn't easily detect him. That's why we always need to be vigilant. We must be circumspect in order to unveil the devil wherever he lurks around us. He is a cannibal; he only feeds on human beings and he does that by first injecting fears into them through his counterfeit roaring and then pouncing on them with his tempting and trying claws.

Turning your back against the devil is not an option; he must be resisted in order to be restricted from devouring you. The resistance must be steadfastly done with the consistency of faith until the game is over on this side of eternity.

As long as we live in this present age, Satan will always fight a child of God. The reason is simply because he knows he's doomed to eternal damnation and, therefore, wants as many people as possible to go to hell with him. And, because of his insatiable destructive appetite, he fights with all his artillery, wiles and schemes.

One of the best ways to handle Satan is to refuse him a foothold in your life. He should always be resisted. In Ephesians 4:27 NKJV, Paul admonishes all believers not to, *"Give place to the devil."* If Satan is given an inch, he will take more than a yard. He loves to take territories and raise them down.

Jesus was quick to discern Satan's scheme when Peter started forbidding Jesus from going to the cross (which the main purpose of Christ's coming to the world). Jesus was almost militant in rebuking the spirit speaking through Peter even though He had just commended him for recognizing him as the Son of God. The devil can speak or come through anyone at any time without them even knowing they are already on his payroll. A good illustration of this is the account of Jesus identifying Satan as the voice behind Peter's attempt to discourage Him from going to the cross. In response, *"Jesus turned and looked at his disciples, he rebuked Peter. 'Get behind me, Satan!' he said. 'You do not have in mind the concerns of God, but merely human concerns'"* (Mark 8:33, NIV).

We can resist Satan by surrendering our lives, properties and circumstances to God, pleading the blood of Jesus Christ, getting rid of idols or satanic images and symbols in our lives and homes, confessing the Word of God, living holy and praising God always.

PRAYER SHOTS:

1. I refuse to give the devil any foothold in my life and properties.
2. Arise, O Lord, on my behalf and let all my enemies be scattered.
3. Abba Father, please deliver me from the strongholds of the evil one.

DAY

4

KEEP THANKING GOD

TEXT: 1 THESSALONIANS 5:18 NKJV

"IN EVERYTHING GIVE THANKS; FOR THIS IS THE WILL OF
GOD IN CHRIST JESUS FOR YOU."

KEY NUGGET: **Thanksgiving is God's perfect plan for you! Make
it a habit!**

My life is reflective of the glory, the grace, and the goodness of God.
God has been so good to me and I cannot thank him enough. If we all take
some time to think deeply, we will find reasons to thank God and that,
thoroughly. Everybody has a story to tell! Looking back on my own life, I
can remember some of the things God has done in my life:

I was once left for dead but got resurrected to life by our great God.

I was once told I could never make it, but God turned my circumstance
around.

I was once abandoned but my God never forsook me.

I was once told I could not get married, but I've been blessed with a
wonderful wife.

My ability to have children was once questioned, but I'm now blessed
with four children.

I am enjoying His grace of ease daily.

I am not consumed by the consumer mentality of the 21st century because of His mercies that I enjoy every day.

God has kept and spared my life over the years because I have escaped many accidents.

God has always come to my defense and protection.

He placed such a high premium on my life by sending His only begotten Son to die for my sins.

A psychology professor passed a white paper with a dot at the center of the page round his class and asked the students if they could spot anything on the paper, but they were all convinced there was nothing on the paper. He then pointed out the dot on the paper and because this exercise was one of the students' continuous assessment tests, they all missed the mark. They all failed the test simply because they missed the dot.

There are people who miss the marks of greatness because they overlooked the seemingly negligible dots of God's goodness. It is gratitude for these dots that often attracts the big marks in life. Gratitude is seen as the attitude of great men. Arrogant people forget to thank God when they are successful, and the ignorant ones refuse to give thanks in challenging times. A grateful heart gives thanks to the Lord in all situations whether the times are good or otherwise.

A man was complaining to God for having only one pair of shoes until he met a man who had no legs giving gratitude to God for being alive! People find it easier to complain about what they don't have and forget to be grateful for the things they have.

Thanksgiving should not be relegated to just national holidays, church programs or an annual family ritual; it should be acknowledged as the will of God for us all in Christ Jesus. Sometimes it seems difficult to identify the will of God in certain circumstances and, consequently, we fear taking the wrong steps. However, giving thanks to the Lord is surely the will of God in all circumstances. Giving thanks to God is always relevant because he daily loads us with benefits. If we are thoughtful, we will always be thankful.

A thousand tongues are never enough to give thanks to God, and neither is there enough days in a year to recount all that he has done for us.

I strongly advise you to pause and take a moment to recount all that God has done for you. Thanking God always opens you up to greater blessings from our loving Father. Hannah thanked God for giving her Samuel and God blessed her with five other children. Of the ten lepers that were healed, only the Samaritan who returned to give thanks was pronounced whole. He was completely freed of all ailments and afflictions (see Luke 17:11-19 NKJV).

So, in everything, give thanks.

PRAYER SHOTS:

1. Lord, I thank you for every day of my life.
2. I give thanks to God who daily loads me with heavenly blessings in Christ Jesus.
3. Blessed be God for His favour, grace and mercies which are renewed every morning.

DAY

THE GIFT OF GOD

TEXT: 2 CORINTHIANS 9:15 NKJV

"THANKS BE TO GOD FOR HIS INDESCRIBABLE GIFT!"

KEY NUGGET: **God's astonishing gift is far too great and overwhelming for words! Response determines value!**

Our God is a great Giver. He gives good and perfect gifts to His children. Jesus Christ, the only begotten Son of God, is the best gift given to man. Through the gift of Jesus, we have power beyond measure (Ephesians 3:20 NKJV), total freedom (John 8:32 NKJV), strength (Philippians 4:13 NKJV), new life (John 3:16 NKJV), wisdom (1 Corinthians 1:24 NKJV), peace (Isaiah 9:6 NKJV), rest (Matthew 11:28 NKJV), and many more.

Our response to God's gift will show the value we place on it. There are times we have been given gifts by loved ones and we don't value them probably because they are not in keeping with our expectations or we are ignorant of their value. Some gifts have even been discarded or passed on to others just because they don't hold any value to us or cannot meet our needs.

Sometime ago, a very wealthy man was approached by a homeless woman who expected him to give her some money. Contrary to her expectation, the wealthy man asked his servant to fill a bag with foodstuffs and gave it to her. The woman was also instructed not to return for alms again, but to go home and cook for her family. This woman reluctantly took the foodstuffs and headed home in utter displeasure. On her way home, and still filled with anger, she decided to give the foodstuffs to another destitute in dire need. When this other destitute got home to cook, she found a cheque of ten thousand dollars in the foodstuff bag neatly kept in an envelope.

This discovery turned her life around and bounced her back on a clean state. A few months later, the homeless lady met the destitute in the neighbourhood looking restored. She curiously asked how she overcame her woes. You can imagine her devastation when she found out the content of foodstuff, she despised was what turned another person's life around.

The same gift despised by the homeless woman was welcomed by the destitute. The homeless woman had contact with the gift but rejected it without checking the contents because it was not packaged according to her expectation. God often delivers His gifts to mankind in unusual packages and in unexpected places.

The sign given to the wise men from the East who came to worship baby Jesus was that he would be seen in a smelly manger, wrapped in swaddling clothes (see Luke 2:12 NKJV). God's gifts usually come wrapped in discouraging containers until you unfold the content.

Only God knows how many gifts of people, opportunities, revelations and endowments we treated with dishonor simply because they appear crude? The Samaritan woman in the Bible had the rare privilege of conversing alone with Jesus but failed to recognize Him as the gift of God for man's salvation. Instead, she questioned Jesus' request for water and almost lost the opportunity to be redeemed (see John 4:4-26 NKJV). However, God, in His mercy, helped this woman to encounter Jesus Christ, His greatest gift to mankind.

One unique feature of the gift of God is that it often beyond description and does not always bear supernatural labels or descriptions that we may easily identify. This is probably one of the reasons why people lose out or failed to appreciate the gifts of God. We must learn to always thank God for his gifts irrespective of their size.

The Saviour of the world came as a baby but the visiting wise men were grateful to God for such a gift to mankind so much so that they went through a harrowing desert journey to worship him. You never know what is hidden in that little package God sent to you! Just go ahead and thank Him for it anyway. We should also respond to the gifts of God through Christ by believing his sacrifices on the cross of Calvary to redeem man back to God. We should remember his mission of wanting to reconcile all of mankind to God the Father.

We must be involved in the work of soul winning by shining our light to this dark and dying world. In Matthew 5:14-15 NKJV, Jesus said, *"You are the light of the world. A city that is set on a hill cannot be hidden. Nor do they light a lamp and put it under a basket, but on a lamp stand, and it gives light to all who are* in the house."

Value God's abundant gifts and display their value by reflecting it on all that you do because you have been justified by grace through faith in the redemptive work of Christ.

PRAYER SHOTS:

1. My Father in heaven, I thank you for the gift of Jesus Christ.
2. Lord, give me the grace to shine the light of your glorious gospel.
3. I receive the power to be a true witness of Jesus Christ.

DAY

6

HOW OLD ARE YOU?

TEXT: PSALM 90:12 NKJV

"So teach us to number our days, That we may gain a heart of wisdom."

KEY NUGGET: **Seek wisdom to interpret your life correctly and make a difference!**

Where I come from, we're usually reluctant to reveal our age when asked as it is often kept a secret and seen as personal. Some are scared to reveal their age because they felt their life's achievements are not commensurate with their age. I also found it scary when I turned 50 as it suddenly dawned on me how little time I have left on earth.

For example, having completed primary school 40 years ago, I discovered that adding forty years to my age makes it 90 years. This new reality made me appreciate Jacob's sentiment when he responded to Pharaoh's question in Genesis 47:8-9 KJV:

"And Pharaoh said unto Jacob, How old art thou? And Jacob said unto Pharaoh, The days of the years of my pilgrimage are an hundred and thirty years: few and evil have the days of the years of my life been, and have not attained unto

THE DAYS OF THE YEARS OF THE LIFE OF MY FATHERS IN
THE DAYS OF THEIR PILGRIMAGE."

As far as Jacob was concerned, the majority of his days on earth were unpleasant. Perceiving life the way Jacob did can only get us exhausted and burnt out before our sojourn on earth is over. It seems like Jacob was already bent and broken before he reached the age of his fathers.

One of the basic needs of life is to learn the value of each day. A lot of people pay a fortune to be financially literate; others pay through their noses for professional literacy while some others enroll for fashion literacy. However, few people ever learn to place the right value on each day of their lives before they die. For any day of our lives to count before God, it must have been lived intentionally and definitely for His purpose. It is only the days we spend making a godly impact that can count for eternity.

People celebrate many years on earth and throw massive birthday parties but they can hardly point out any of those years that have eternal value. We need to constantly ask ourselves how many days of our lives we allow to go wasted each year. Without the conscious effort to invest our days in impact-making choices, we will always take the wrong steps and make unwise decisions. The heart that gains wisdom is the heart that reflects deeply in the passing nature of the privilege called day. Our years are only as important as the value of each day within each year.

Our time on earth is brief so we need to redeem the time because the days we live in are evil. We must not procrastinate but should always endeavour to live a life of legacy. We need to make an impact and add value to the life of others.

We should live our lives with eternity in view. Death is a leveler and since we're not invincible or immortal, we must make hay while time lasts. The end will eventually come as we age and, the truth of the matter is, death cannot be prevented by medicine.

With these in mind, the thought of our age should drive us to action in serving humanity, making peace with everyone, creating memories with loved ones, establishing legacies, and passing on our wisdom and experiences.

Let us be like David who served his generations doing the will of God (see Acts 13:36 KJV).

In answering how old you are, always remember these three questions:

- Where did I come from?
- Where am I going?
- What will be said about me or written on my epitaph?

PRAYER SHOTS:

1. Lord, please increase my passion for lost souls.
2. My life will not be a waste in Jesus' name. My life will matter in my generation.
3. My Father in heaven, please teach me to number my days so that I can apply my heart to wisdom.

DAY

7

DON'T STAY AT THE BUS STOP

TEXT: EPHESIANS 4:31-32 NIV

"Get rid of all bitterness, rage and anger, brawling and slander, along with every form of malice. Be kind and compassionate to one another, forgiving each other, just as in Christ, God forgave you."

KEY NUGGET: The bus is ready to move; get onboard!

A young man was getting married some years ago so his wedding preparations were in top gear. A few days to the wedding, his mother paid him a visit at his new apartment where he was going to start his marital life. When she got there, she noticed a heap of refuse at the entrance and some sacks of abandoned garbage in his backyard. She wondered why someone starting a new life would accommodate such a volume of old wastes. So, she persuaded him to get rid of the garbage in preparation to welcoming his new bride into a clean and fresh environment.

It is usually difficult to attract a new life without getting rid of an old one. Many people are delayed in experiencing freshness in life because they are stuck to the garbage of their past and litter their emotional corridors with relics of the wastes from their past. Yet, they hope to have a new experience and a breath of fresh air. You cannot eat your cake and still have it.

The courage to get rid of wrong things is essential to creating room for the right things. When we summon the boldness to rid ourselves of bitterness, rage, anger, brawling, slander and malice, etc., we would have cleared the drainage of our lives of communicable diseases and demolished the habitation of spiritual infections. Consequently, our hearts would then be able to handle kindness, we become compassionate and forgiveness comes easily, regardless of the hurt. An exit for bitterness creates an entrance for sweetness.

The things we were enjoined to get rid of are simply life's bus stops and not a residence. It often fascinates me to observe the way people rush for public mass transport in some cities around the world. I noticed that people only transit through bus stops because it is not a place of abode. Staying put at the bus stop without boarding any of the buses would appear strange and even suspicious in some situations. Staying at the bus stop in this illustration is like refusing to let go of hurts, offences, emotional wounds, etc. We need to forgive, get on the bus of pardon, and move on with our lives.

We sometimes get used to wrong habits to a point where we begin to view those attempting to help us get rid of them as our adversaries. It is difficult to change the way one has always reacted to offences, especially when it has become second nature. Some people even boast of their bitterness and anger as something they inherited from their ancestors. We need a self-cleansing sanitation to rid our lives of emotional and spiritual germs.

Joseph was sold into slavery by his siblings, maligned by his master's wife and was sent to prison for an offence he never committed. While in the prison, he was forgotten by the King's Butler whose dream he had interpreted. Despite all these, he ended being the Prime Minister of Egypt. As Prime Minister, he had the opportunity to get even for the wrongs done to him by both his siblings and Potiphar's wife, but he let go and let God. He forgave all and never remained at that bus stop!

Joseph narrated a short version of his life's story to his siblings who had expected him to remain at the bus stop of unforgiveness. Contrary to their expectations, his response to them was, *"As for you, ye thought evil against me; but God meant it unto good, to bring to pass, as it is this day, to save much people alive"* (Genesis 50:20 KJV).

He understood that his brother's intention was inferior to what God purposed to achieve in his life. He saw his brothers' evil agenda towards him as a divine vehicle to his destiny. One of the ways we can get rid of bitterness and anger is to ascribe the overriding result of people's bitterness against us to God's goodness. While Joseph's brothers thought they were selling him into slavery, it turned out that they were sending him to his place of purpose. God's ultimate goal was to preserve him so he could serve humanity and set a standard of leadership in the face of daunting scarcity.

You are created for upward and forward motion, so don't allow bitterness to tie you down to one spot.

PRAYER SHOTS:

1. My Father, please uproot every root and seed of bitterness from my life.
2. Lord, enlarge my heart's capacity to forgive with ease.
3. I receive the Spirit of Jesus Christ in order to love the unlovable and to forgive all.

DAY

CONTROL YOUR ATMOSPHERE

TEXT: 1 PETER 5:7 TPT

"POUR OUT ALL YOUR WORRIES AND STRESS UPON HIM AND LEAVE THEM THERE, FOR HE ALWAYS TENDERLY CARES FOR YOU."

KEY NUGGET: **Take control of your situations and leave your burdens at His feet.**

Atmospheric and environmental pressure can push a lot of people out of control because they have not learned to subdue their souls. Ships don't sink because of turbulent waters unless the water gets into the ship. For the ship to keep floating the water must not be permitted to flood the inside. Many things often happen around our lives that are beyond our control, however, we must learn to guard our emotional atmosphere against these adverse environmental conditions.

To achieve this, we must trust the Lord with our worries. Many have allowed too much space in their hearts for worry. They accommodate, feed and nurture their worries like a pet. They have created shelves and wardrobes of worries in their minds. Some even take their worries to the Lord in prayer but failed to leave them at His feet. As soon as they're done praying, they pick up from where they left off; running helter-skelter with their problems all over again. They always want instant intervention and if there is a slight delay in divine response, they take try to find their own solutions.

Worries don't evaporate or vanish away so, it's always to leave them with the Lord.

Worries can be very toxic to the heart as they break down the walls of hope and demolish the fortresses of joy. Many people have developed unnecessary terminal diseases because of worry. Some people have worried all their lives so much that they feel odd when there's nothing to worry about.

On a visit to an agricultural research Institution in Africa, a young man observed that even during dry seasons the farmlands were always green and wet. In youthful curiosity, he asked the farm manager how they managed to keep their crops green even when the environment was dry and dusty. The farm manager smiled and said, "We control our atmosphere here." We must all learn to control our emotional, spiritual and mental atmospheres. We must be properly irrigated with a regular supply of divine inspirations before reacting to situations.

In Genesis 26:1-33 KJV, Isaac controlled his farmland during the famine by digging wells. While others responded by waiting for the rain to fall, Isaac dug deeper beyond the shallow surface to generate a steady supply of water for his crops. Little wonder he reaped a hundredfold in the same year he planted his seeds.

Some people would have been devastated while the famine persisted and be looking to blame God, their parents, governments, and even their race for their calamity. But for Isaac, he took control of the situation by reaching deep for the water underground. Anytime life puts you under pressure, refrain from losing your temper or be full of complaints and negativity. Self-control in tough situations is such a powerful tool for controlling our atmosphere.

We should cultivate an attitude of always praising God in tough times, to give Him thanks even when things are not working according to expectation.

Your needs may not always be met from the usual sources, but when you cast your worries on the Lord, you cannot be stranded. Remember God's sources are manifold; therefore, He can instruct the depths to deliver when it seems like nothing is coming from the heights. Self-control is the prime of virtues. We often fall for the devil's wiles because when we face a blockade, we conclude in our minds that there's no way out and thus find ourselves unconsciously agreeing with his suggestions and lies.

It is not unnatural to worry, especially when faced with fears and threats, but it is supernatural to be worry-free because there is peace and comfort in entrusting our concerns with the Shepherd of our souls.

PRAYER SHOT:

1. Father in heaven, let your peace be assured in my life.
2. Lord, let me experience your stability and serenity in every area of my life.
3. I will rest in you Lord.

DAY

9

LOOK AHEAD

TEXT: JEREMIAH 29:11 NKJV

"For I know the thoughts that I think toward you, says the Lord, thoughts of peace and not of evil, to give you a future and a hope."

KEY NUGGET: **Don't wait for someone else to pick up your broken pieces; pick them up yourself, stay future-oriented and look towards your glorious future.**

In counseling a young woman, I was baffled by the fact that she kept insisting she would never forgive her father who had abused her in the past. She was still being tormented by her past and was not willing to go beyond its borders. Some people are so obsessed with the past that they cannot imagine the future. We must learn to outgrow the negative treatments and unpleasant circumstances that we have or may still encounter.

Look ahead: there are lots of opportunities beyond the familiar or the usual. Don't be trapped into the snare of mediocrity or your comfort zone. Rather, turn your challenges into experiences that will make you a blessing to others who are still trying to navigate their way through such challenges. When confronted with unpleasant circumstance, we should understand that God's presence and promises present to comfort us so we can also be able to encourage and comfort others. Challenges are designed to properly frame us into people who by virtue of our own experiences can give assistance to others who are faced with similar ordeals.

Learn to piece the broken parts together and move on to the glorious future ahead of you. Be like Ruth who stayed with Naomi, her mother-in-law. Naomi experienced the loss of three men in her life: her husband and their two sons, one of which was Ruth's husband. So, Naomi decided to depart from Moab and return home. She called her two daughters-in-law, Ruth and Orpah, and admonished them to go back to their people.

Ruth, however, decided to cleave to Naomi and follow her home. She chose to remain loyal to her late husband's family and looked ahead to a future full of opportunities. She eventually got married to Boaz and produced a son in the lineage of our Lord and Saviour, Jesus Christ. We can confidently look ahead when we understand that God always has us on His mind. Some people tend to interpret their future by their past without considering the vitality of God's intentions for them.

God knows the thoughts He thinks towards you, but the question is: "Do you know those thoughts?" To be ignorant of what God is doing in your life is to open the door for temptation and compromise. God never thinks of troubles and evil towards you. He cannot imagine evil against His children. The challenge is often our inabilities to understand that whatever negative experiences and paths He allows to go through are intended for our ultimate good. Sometimes, it may be difficult for us to understand the present until the future comes.

Sometime ago, a woman was frying plantains for her hungry 2-year-old daughter. While the plantain was freshly extracted from the hot oil, the child cried for a bite and because the food was too hot, her mother did not yield. And, even though the child began to throw tantrums, this woman would not risk giving her the hot plantains. To the 2-year-old, her mother was being mean, but the reality is that this woman was only trying to save her from a potential harm.

Oftentimes, we also fall victim to the same mindset through our limited understanding of what God is up to in our lives! We tend to always crave what we're equipped to handle. We want to ingest what our immature guts cannot digest. Sometimes, all we can see are fried plantains and are oblivious to the fact that they may be too hot for our mouths and we may suffer burns.

Only heaven knows how many injuries we have inflicted on our marital, ministerial and spiritual tongues because we want to eat what we believe God has prepared for us but failed to realize we're not ready to handle them yet. We must realize that until God reveals His plans to us as humans, they remain His thoughts and known only to him.

That gap in time is often difficult for man to patiently wait and trust God with. In the same vein, the good that God is working for us may appear like a puzzle and in contrast to what we expect, but in the end it comes together. Sadly, many people are not able to endure to the end and wait to see the puzzles come together.

Life doesn't make meaning by us consulting the dictionary of the past; it only makes sense when we allow the One who holds the future to define it for us, and that, in His own time.

It is unwise to hastily judge how a thing will end simply by seeing how it began.

PRAYER SHOT:

1. Father, please open my eyes to see the future you have for me.
2. Lord, remove every cataract obstructing my vision.
3. I shall begin to recognize opportunities in the land in the name of Jesus.

DAY

10

WHERE ARE YOU?

TEXT: JOHN 3:16 NKJV

"FOR GOD SO LOVED THE WORLD THAT HE GAVE HIS
ONLY BEGOTTEN SON, THAT WHOEVER BELIEVES IN HIM
SHOULD NOT PERISH BUT HAVE EVERLASTING LIFE."

KEY NUGGET: **Be at peace with God and you will gain access to the peace of God!**

I am always intrigued by the Global Positioning Satellite (GPS) system because as helpful it is; it is also prone to errors especially when driving through unfamiliar areas. As a result, some people have been taken to the wrong locations. So, as good as the GPS is, it incapable of guiding you to peace or to the purpose of God for your life.

When God saw that Adam and Eve had messed up, He first called out to them by asking, "Where are you?" (Genesis 3:9 NKJV). In the same vein, before God can do anything about who you are now, you to first confess where you are to Him. He's not concerned about the whereabouts of those who are properly positioned where He wants them to be. God gives names to places and people in line with their purposes so, you need also need to align who you are and where you are with what God wants you to do.

A man can be alive and still be missing in God's scheme of things. God is still asking man the same question He asked the first Adam: "Where are you"? Wrong actions and decisions are like aircrafts wandered off the radar. They always lead to the untraceable places before they eventually crash. To be located or relocated, we need to stop running around and away from God. There is only one way to have access to and fellowship with God, and that way is Jesus; He is the Way, the Truth and the Life (see John 14:6 NKJV).

We cannot afford to ignore the love of God and the kind of intensity with which He loves us. It is amazing to see the boundless love of God shown in Christ Jesus. We must always be grateful to know that we're included in the precious list of God's beloveds. It is easy for men to love people of their race, background or denominational inclination, but some folks have it so bad that they find it even impossible to love themselves. Yet, despite our wrongs and weaknesses, God still loves the whole world. Life cannot be better for anyone apart from Christ.

God expects us to have a relationship with Him. After Adam and Eve sinned and hid themselves, God came seeking them out. He desired to have a close relationship with them, but they hid from Him because their sin exposed their nakedness. Sin will keep anyone running away from the light of joy and peace into the thick darkness of fear and misery.

Whoever believes in Jesus Christ is embraced by God regardless of their social status or moral upbringing. You do not need any special training to believe in God's love through Christ Jesus. You don't need a special course to start your journey of faith with God. There is no need for a special academic qualification or financial donation gaining access into the loving arms of Jesus.

The first benefit of believing the finished work of Jesus at the cross is eternal life. It must be clear to us that humanity was doomed in Adam, but Christ brought the exception to that rule by His death and resurrection. There is still room for you to run into the everlasting arms of Grace. Some have perished and some will perish, not because they're poor or because they don't go to a church, but because they refuse to believe and accept Jesus as Lord over their lives. Believing in Jesus does not just save you from perishing; it also preserves you with eternal life.

No human life can be preserved outside of time, not even that of the rich and the wealthy. If it were possible, billionaires would have secured and insured themselves against death. However, eternal life cannot be bought with money. You may be having fun with your current ungodly lifestyle but know for sure that you will soon be gone and forgotten on this earth. The only secured life is everlasting life through Christ Jesus!

The system of this world cannot give you rest. Earthly governments cannot provide rest. It is only when we come to God that we have rest. Jesus affirmed this truth in Matthew 11:28-30 KJV when he said, *"Come unto me, all ye that labour and are heavy laden and I will give you rest. Take my yoke upon you, and learn of me; for I am meek and lowly in heart: and ye shall find rest unto your souls. For my yoke is easy, and my burden is light."*

To find your way to God, you must come to Jesus by faith. You cannot keep going on the wrong path and expect to find peace with God. The junction of faith is a U-turn where going changes into coming. You must turn your back on where you were facing and head in the direction towards the open arms of Jesus. Until you meet Him, your labour in life will be straddled with heavy burdens. There is no easy yoke for the unbeliever. His worries, concerns, fears and anxieties come with heavy weights of uncertainties and, no assistance is granted to him until Christ takes over the weight from him.

PRAYER SHOT:

1. Father, please guide me through the journey of life.
2. Let every giant on my way fall after the order of Goliath.
3. I receive the insight of God to navigate the complexities of this world, in Jesus' name.

DAY 11

SELF DEVELOPMENT

TEXT: PROVERBS 18:15 NKJV

"The heart of the prudent acquires knowledge,
And the ear of the wise seeks knowledge."

KEY NUGGET: **Pay premium on self-development, regardless of the cost!**

Many people in life have stopped growing and they just refuse to improve themselves. One of the major differences between humans and animals is the capacity to acquire and refine knowledge'. Animals are primitive in knowledge acquisition and that's the reason why they are subdued and controlled by man despite the numerical and physical strength of many of them. Knowledge is so crucial in the day and time we live that being ignorant is considered harmful. Hosea 4:6 KJV says, *"My people are destroyed for lack of knowledge."* Many nations and people of the world are in ruin, not because they lack mineral resources or natural endowments, but because they refuse to develop their human capital and capacity.

Imagine a continent plagued over the years with malaria infection because they lack world-class research centers for developing anti-malarial drugs or eradicating mosquitos (a vehicle for the plasmodium pathogen). Most anti-malaria drugs are either manufactured outside the African continent or indirectly imported through intellectually researched and developed prescriptions.

Many people pray against the lack of money and opportunities, however, the real lack they ought to tackle is that of knowledge. The apathy being exhibited towards knowledge today (even by believers) is worrisome. The level of mental decay is alarming, and one could almost get nauseated at the degree of ignorance being spewed out from the pulpits and celebrated on the pews.

The ignorance of government in some nations has jeopardized the lives of their citizens and sent more children to their early graves than any war could have. The disintegration of homes and families due to parental ignorance of requisite knowledge in some couples is almost beyond articulation.

The nature of the heart determines what a man invests his time and energy in. You cannot change a man's priority when it comes to his acquisition except you first change his heart. It takes a prudent heart; a heart that diligently and objectively pants after knowledge. Knowledge is not innate and cannot be acquired by birth.

There is a price tag associated with the acquisition of the right kind of knowledge. The unwillingness of many to pay this price is what tends to deter them from acquiring knowledge. Many people will rather spend money to acquire ceremonial uniforms and gadgets than enroll in self-development programs and training. Little wonder they end up being preys of misinformation as attested to by the popular saying: "What you do not know may kill you!" Self-development includes reading, training, retraining, attending seminars, conferences, developing new skills, etc.

One of the ways a prudent heart acquires knowledge is through listening. The ears of the wise are sensitive enough to receive knowledge by paying attention to information from reliable sources. Many people are ignorant because they don't know how to listen. They are good at talking but very poor at listening to what others have to say. Some people's ears are only inclined to gossips, rumours, slanders, falsehoods and such like.

Invest time in seeking out new information; the kind that produces revelation which ultimately produces a revolution of the mind. Through reading and understanding of books, Daniel was able to shorten the captivity of his people (see Daniel 9:2-27 KJV). His understanding propelled him to fast and pray to God for the deliverance of his nation. Many people have perpetuated their oppression and subjection, not because of the power of their oppressors, but because their mental capacity is too weak to agitate for their freedom.

Don't be stuck in the wrong and old ways of doing things. Tradition is usually a hindrance to transition. Your skills might be outdated, and you might just be out of tune with the beats of the time. Be open to new learning so that you don't lose your relevance. Knowledge should be our constant pursuit on this side of eternity because our current reality is a mere reflection of the future. In this present fast paced world where ideas are invented and dispensed to solve problems at the speed of light, a man who loses his grip on knowledge may drown in the sea of frustration. If you assume education is expensive, a trial of ignorance will make you see otherwise.

Paul, the apostle, was an ardent reader even in the twilight of his life on earth. He wrote to Timothy, his protégé, in 2 Timothy 4:13 NIV, requesting him to *"Bring the cloak that I left with Carpus at Troas, and my scrolls, **especially the parchments**."*

`If you were in a situation where you must salvage your properties from a disaster, would your books and parchments be of priority? If you were to ask a dear friend of yours to bring you, your spouse or your parents something precious from a long journey, would books be on your list? It is not surprising that Paul was not only able to achieve great things but was relevant throughout his entire life on earth. You too can, if you place a great premium on self-development no matter the cost.

PRAYER SHOTS:

1. Father in heaven, please increase my knowledge of you and your Word.
2. Lord my God, please enlighten my darkness.
3. I commend myself to the Holy Spirit for training, leading and counselling.

DAY

12

DADDY, CALL ME BACK

TEXT: JEREMIAH 33:3 NKJV

"Call to Me, and I will answer you, and show you
great and mighty things, which you do not know."

KEY NUGGET: Choose to open the door and feast with Him.

I travel a lot as a result of my ministerial involvement. In one of my
journeys away from my family, as soon as I settled at my destination, I
decided to call my family though I was conscious of the fact that they
would probably be in bed due to time difference. I was able to talk to those
who were still awake.

However, my last baby who was asleep when I called woke up and
sent me a text saying, "Daddy, call me back." I did of course and she was
so happy to hear from me.

Sometimes, we miss the accurate timing of God's call about where
we should be and where we should go. However, as soon as we realize our
errors, we must endeavour to retrace our steps and request guidance from
the Lord. God will not give you another instruction beyond your last point
of obedience.

CALL TO ME:

Many people are familiar with the numbers of their phone contacts than they are with God's direct line in prayers. Some would rather that God initiate a call to them whereas, God has been waiting on their calls. It is amazing how much time and resources some folks invest in calling their business or emotional partners and in maintaining their professional connections, but never consider investing such in calling the out to the Lord. When some believers fall sick, their natural reaction is to call their physician rather than calling on the Lord. When people's marriages are falling apart, a call to their parents seems more expedient to them than telling the Lord about it.

Sadly, most of the people we count on in distress may not even come through for us due to their challenges or limitations. Most of us have had experiences with unanswered calls because the people we call are either unavailable or unable to answer their calls. Some won't even take the calls because they are so used to problem calls that they can always predict the reasons for such calls. On the contrary, God already promised His children that He will answer, even before they call with stringent conditions or time restrictions. You can always call on Him in the wee hours of the night and He will answer. We are subject to limitations in certain circumstances until we call on God in prayers. There are things we won't know unless God reveals them to us. Men's kindness often always comes with strings attached, but only God can truly show us kindness beyond our imaginations without making us feel indebted.

There are things that science cannot reveal nether can telescopes, microscopes, scanners or laser beams; only God can see everything. Some realities hidden to the natural man and only God can unveil them to whosoever He wishes.

God is willing to communicate with you, but you must open your heart to Him.

In Matthew 14:30 KJV, Peter did the impossible, defied the odds, operated in the supernatural and walked on water! He was able to handle gravity just like Jesus did, but when Peter *"Saw that the wind was boisterous, he was afraid; and beginning to sink he cried out, saying, 'Lord, save me!'"*

Peter began to sink the moment he started paying attention to the threats of the wind. Part of the devil's scheme is to distract us from our faith in order to douse and weaken our hope. We've all probably had those moments when things go contrary to our expectations and we begin to lose confidence in the Word of God. Some things happen in life that overwhelms us with fear and we first lose courage and then our faith. An African proverb says, "When a child gets to a fearful place, he will give in to fear". The wind of life can often get so loud that it can draw our attention away from our focus.

Peter's fear terminated his strong walk on water and resulted in the start of his sinking. When we stop walking by faith, we start sinking in fear. When faith is turned off, fear comes on. What saved Peter from sinking was that he cried out, "Lord save me" just in time. His call came when he began to sink not after he sank. Many times, we have sunk into shame and errors because we failed to cry out to the Lord when the problems were still controllable. We often assume we can handle things on our own until we pass the privilege of being rescued on time.

Peter cry to the Lord was a precise call for help. Stop bottling things up until the damage becomes irreparable. Get on your knees and pray; call unto Jesus and be assured He will answer and show you the way out of your stranded corner.

Revelation 3:20 NIV says, *"Here I am! I stand at the door and knock. If anyone hears my voice and opens the door, I will come in and eat with that person, and they with me."*

PRAYER SHOTS:

1. Father, please deepen my longing for you.
2. Lord, fill me up to overflow.
3. Shepherd of my soul, I give you full control of my life.

13

GOD'S TITLE DEEDS

TEXT: *1 CORINTHIANS 3:21 NKJV

"THEREFORE LET NO ONE BOAST IN MEN. FOR ALL THINGS ARE YOURS."

KEY NUGGET: God's gifts are freely given and all we have to do is accept it!

A wealthy man who died had a clause in his will where his only son is entitled to just one item from all his assets while the rest is willed to his servant. This news rattled the son who wondered why his father would leave only one item for him and leave the rest of his estate to a servant. As if that was not enough, he was also told he had only two weeks to make his choice known.

Before the appointed day, the servant had gone ahead to retain the services of musicians, caterers, and other vendors to celebrate his sudden windfall. Meanwhile, the late man's son was so depressed and confused at his situation that he decided to seek the wise counsel of one of his father's close friends. When this father's friend heard the story, he chuckled and simply advised the son to select the servant since he was also part of his late father's property. This young man left elated after receiving this old man's wise counsel.

On the appointed day, there was a large gathering of people waiting anxiously to hear this young man's choice. His father's servant, who is now arrayed in ceremonial attire, was also on standby with his entourage of friends. To the surprise of everyone, the son pointed at the servant and declared him as his only choice of his late father's property. The servant was dumbfounded when it suddenly dawned on him that he's also part of the late man's estate and, by implication, he now belongs to his master's son.

This late man's son would have missed out in life, blamed his father for his woes and live miserably. The father's intention was for his son to inherit his estate, but he also wanted this son to make the right choice in doing so.

Oftentimes, it may appear like little was left of our inheritance in God's will for us. This mindset discourages many from seeking counsel in the right places that would help them make the right decisions and unlock God's promises. Many Christians want God's miracle without following His principles for living.

God has no problems releasing all He has for us, but there are conditions He has set for us to lay hold on them. We must always be willing to seek and embrace the right counsels which can lead us into God's eternal truths and plans for us. The love that God has for His children is so strong that He gave His only begotten Son for our salvation and gives us all things to enjoy.

There are phenomenal and great blessings from God the father. He has prepared unique things for us. God's incredible promises for His children are contained in His Word and we can appropriate these promises into our lives by obeying what the word says.

In 1 Corinthians 2:9 NIV, we read, *"As it is written: 'what no eye has seen, what no ear has heard, and what no human mind has conceived' — the things God has prepared for those who love him."*

God's intentions are contained in His written word so we should not be in doubt, because God is committed to what is written therein. No one in hell can undo what God has written. God's promises are not things awarded by international companies for meritorious services. They are things He personally prepared for those who love Him. Hence, loving God is fundamental to getting all that God has in store for you. The question for you and me then is: "Do you love the Lord?" Are there fruits in our lives to demonstrate our love for the Lord? Loving the Lord is a prerequisite to receiving what He has prepared for us.

Our God is a great giver; nobody gives like Him. He freely gives lot of wonderful things to us and He gives them unconditionally. When God gives, He gives to the fullest. He releases more than we can ever ask or imagine in our wildest dreams. Paul's prayer in Ephesians 3:19-20 NIV is for the believer, *"To know this love that surpasses knowledge—that you may be filled to the measure of all the fullness of God. Now to him who is able to do immeasurably more than all we ask or imagine, according to his power that is at work within us."*

With faith in God and His words, we can enjoy the best of God. Through the blood of Jesus shed at the cross of Calvary, we are granted access to divine wealth, health, joy, peace, protection, grace, etc.

PRAYER SHOTS:

1. Lord, I thank you for your spiritual blessings in Christ Jesus.
2. My God shall supply all my needs according to His riches in Christ Jesus.
3. I will not lack anything good in Jesus' name.

DAY

14

YOU NEED A FATHER

TEXT: GALATIANS 4:19 NKJV

"MY LITTLE CHILDREN, FOR WHOM I LABOR IN BIRTH
AGAIN UNTIL CHRIST IS FORMED IN YOU."

KEY NUGGET: **Fathers bring strength and stability; don't neglect
the role of your father.**

Fatherhood is the highest honour God bestows on man. When a man
becomes a father; he shares an unusual honour with God. Fatherhood
is critical in shaping a child into the right adult. For Christ to be fully
formed in a child, a spiritually sensitive father must labour over that child
consistently and continually in training and prayers. Today, many children
are spiritually deformed because they lack fatherly influence while others
resist their fathers' labour to have Christ formed in them.

My son was walking through a corridor one day when the light
suddenly went off. He screamed out, "Daddy come and carry me!" Armed
with my little flashlight, I ran out from where I was to fetch him. Though
we both walked through the dark hallway, he was not afraid because I
(his father) was with him. Some of life's passages towards destiny may
be dangerous and frightening to walk through without a father. Quite a
number have aborted their journey into significance because the light they

depended on during the dark moments was switched off and they had no one to call for help.

Education, as important as it is, does not translate to spiritual transformation in a child. An African adage says that a father who sits under a tree can see beyond what a child who climbs the same tree may see. The insight, hindsight and foresight of a father are needed to help a child navigate through the uncharted territories of life.

The clamour for liberty today has robbed many young people of their fathers' roles in shaping their future both spiritually and materially. As soon as some children feel they're old enough, they're quick to rid themselves of any kind of parental control. Some would go as far as choosing higher institutions far away from home just to avoid the roving eyes of their parents. There are students who would rather stay on the campus during the holidays in order to avoid their "controlling" fathers.

You can avoid some errors in life simply by learning important life lessons from the experiences of a good father. You can avoid certain pitfalls if your hind horse learns from the pilot horse. Yes, honest and sincere fathers may be hard to come by in our days, but their scarcity is not proof they don't exist.

Some Christians are convinced that they don't need spiritual fathers because they have the Holy Spirit, so they live on their terms. However, it is evident that to go farther in life, you'll still need a father. A good father invests time and effort to nurture the character of a child. His emphasis is on developing the child's inward man who will subsequently develop into the outward man.

A father provides spiritual covering for his children. Everyone born into this world is a product of a father's seed planted into a mother's womb. Sadly, our world today is full of fatherless people who wander around laden with a lot of issues in their lives because they are lacking certain blessings that only their fathers can release on them. A father is endowed by the Creator to pronounce blessings on his offspring. For example, the blessings bestowed upon Joseph, Ephraim and Manasseh in Genesis 48 had great impacts on their lives and revealed God's mind concerning their destinies.

Good fathers are sensitive to their children's conditions and so ensure these children are brought up with sound godly training. Even nations also need fathers of faith to consult in times in crisis. In 2 Kings 2:19-22 KJV, there was what appears to be a national problem in Jericho, so the leaders visited with Elisha, their spiritual father, and asked him to pronounce blessings on their land in order to reverse the curse placed on their land. Elisha did as they asked, and the curse was removed to this day (read 2 Kings 2:20-21 KJV).

PRAYER SHOTS:

1. Father of all blessings, please bless me and make me fruitful.
2. Lord, let your everlasting arms surround me.
3. I declare that I carry the seeds of greatness as my Heavenly Father, in Jesus' name.

DAY

15

SOWING SEEDS

TEXT: GENESIS 8:22 NKJV

"WHILE THE EARTH REMAINS, SEEDTIME AND HARVEST, COLD AND HEAT, WINTER AND SUMMER, AND DAY AND NIGHT SHALL NOT CEASE."

KEY NUGGET: **The purity of a seed determines its quality; sow sparingly and reap sparingly, sow bountifully and reap bountifully.**

When the Bible declares that something shall not cease, no technology can halt that declaration. The conditions under which the earth operates are ordained by God Himself. For any man to be effective on this earth, he must operate under God's divine and fundamental principles. They represent the pillars on which God founded the earth. Our focus in this section is on the principle of seedtime and harvest.

Some people have ignorantly joined prayer wagons on harvesting. A lot of conferences are held these days by religious organizations on prayers for a quick harvest, but these human ideas are simply in contradiction to God's laid down principles. Seedtime will always precede harvest time. Seedtime is a season when God blesses you with seeds and guides you to different lands of opportunities to sow into. It is when you plant your seeds into arable lands in hope of a future harvest.

This is not the time to expect a harvest, but a time to sow the appropriate seeds. It's not the time for the businessperson to go on vacation or purchase a flashy automobile. No, seedtime is when you sow into your vision, acquire knowledge, and invest in godly relationships or a benevolent cause. A man who wastes his seedtime should not be praying for any harvest. To harvest what you did not sow or where you did not sow is tantamount either to begging or robbery. Many parents desire to harvest peace from the lives of their children in their old age but failed to invest quality time in teaching them important life's values and skills when they were young. Instead, they used the formative years of their children traipsing around the world and ended up reaping a harvest of regrets.

God expects us to serve others and be found faithful in handling other people's businesses so that He can bless our own. You cannot develop apathy for your employer's business and expect commitment from your employees. God has given us all a seedtime as an opportunity for us to design and determine what our harvest will be like.

Many teachers have taught students who later grew up to occupy positions of influence in life, but because of the hatred and brutality with which they treated these children then, they cannot expect to now reap help and kindness from them. Nowadays, some poor people have abandoned their responsibilities to serve with sincerity in pursuit of the wealth of the privileged and, in the process, have strained their divine relationship with God.

When Moses departed, Joshua did not prepare for the mantle of leading God's people to suddenly fall on him the way it did. However, his seedtime was when he faithfully served Moses, encouraged the people to go for what God has promised, and discharged a courageous speech of possibility against the negative mindset of the majority. It is little wonder he was rewarded with the harvest of leading God's people into the Promised Land after collecting the baton from Moses.

Sowing is a responsibility that you can either embrace or ignore, but the consequences of your decisions are inevitable. To preserve your future, you must learn to maximize the present with a good habit of using what you're endowed with for the good of others.

While growing up, I keenly observed my late father separating some good tubers of yam as seeds after every harvest in his farm. It didn't make sense to me then why we had to cut some of our best yams into few pieces and later bury them in the ground for a later harvest. As I grew older, I realized that it had to be done that way for us to reap a good harvest the following year. It was this experience of observing my father that taught me the principle of sowing and reaping.

This world we live in is governed by principles. Anyone who operates with these principles will reap the attending results, whether they're saved or not; particularly the principle of sowing and reaping. God's mandate is that as this earth remains, seedtime and harvest shall never cease.

The seed is usually smaller than the harvest, but you still reap what you sow and that's in proportion to what is sown. How this principle operates is still beyond human comprehension because it is not a mathematical formula; it simply works for those who apply it.

There is no human on earth with nothing to sow as some seeds could be in form of laughter, information, money, good deeds, and so on. For example, Jonathan sowed seeds of love and loyalty to David and the attending harvest was so huge that, even long after Jonathan's demise, his generation after him was still benefiting from its fruits (see 2 Samuel 9 KJV). God also *sowed* His only begotten son as a *seed* in order to harvest many sons in return (see John 3:16 KJV).

Look around you and identify what seeds are available for you to sow; you or your generations after you will end up enjoying the harvest in the end.

PRAYER SHOTS:

1. Father, I ask that you let all my sown seeds be prosperous.
2. Lord, let the seeds I sow today bring harvests that can meet my needs tomorrow.
3. I decree that the seeds I sow today will break down tomorrow's siege in Jesus' name.

DAY

16

DESIRE GRACE

TEXT: 2 CORINTHIANS 12:9 NKJV

AND HE SAID TO ME, "MY GRACE IS SUFFICIENT FOR YOU, FOR MY STRENGTH IS MADE PERFECT IN WEAKNESS." THEREFORE MOST GLADLY I WILL RATHER BOAST IN MY INFIRMITIES, THAT THE POWER OF CHRIST MAY REST UPON ME.

KEY NUGGET: **GRACE prevents us from being slaves to the law, but slaves to His love. God's forgiving capacity is inexhaustible.**

A friend once shared his first-time experience on an elevator and though it was funny, it was also a great illustration of God's grace at work. He narrated that he almost lost his balance the moment he stepped onto the elevator and impulsively tried to climb up like he would a flight of stairs. Right beside him was a young fellow who was apparently familiar with riding elevators said to him, "Sir, let the elevator take you up!" My friend was initially embarrassed when he realized that this young one was able to both calm him down and advised him to not try and do the elevator's job for the elevator.

This experience turned out to be one of my friend's greatest lessons in life. You don't have to struggle for the elevating grace of God; it is His gift to mankind but at the expense of Christ. Let the elevator of God's grace take you up the ladder of possibility and your reality will be exponential.

Many people struggle with their spiritual walk and so they invest a lot of time and effort to be faultless in their character. Some even bind themselves with oaths, promising never to repeat certain bad habits, only to find themselves back in the middle of their past errors repeatedly. You cannot attain the righteousness of God by being religious or ritualistic. Our righteousness rests solely and absolutely on the grace of God.

We can see that God reinforces the certainty of His grace through his Word. Nothing expounds the capacity of God's grace to a believer better than His Word. It was what God spoke to Paul that carried him through the lowest point of his life. This shows that we cannot activate God's grace in ignorance; hence, we must constantly be in tune with His Word for His grace to work for us.

No matter how deep and far the sea of need we swim through, God's grace is sufficient for us to go the distance. A man that trusts in anything else outside of God's grace will be greeted with early disappointment in life. The efficacy of God's grace is embedded in its sufficiency.

Those who think they are strong in one area of their lives or the other cannot experience the very depth of God's grace. The grace God only strengthens the weak; however, God often allows those who trust in their own ability to come to their wit's end before granting them access to His grace. Grace is only supplied where there is a demand. It is not weakness that limits a man, it is his inability to embrace the sufficiency of God's grace and own up to his weaknesses in the flesh.

Grace is God's sufficiency in the life of the believer. Grace was paid for in full at Calvary and the currency was the precious blood of Jesus Christ. The Greek word for grace is *charis*, which means goodwill or God's kindness. Grace is the unmerited, undeserved, and unearned favour and kindness of God. Anything we've been able to do in this life (no matter how basic) is because we are helped by His grace.

Ephesians 2:8-9, Paul highlights the truth that, *"For by grace you have been saved through faith, and that not of yourselves; it is* the gift of God, *not of works, lest anyone should boast."* Once we trust and put our faith in Him (this speaks of salvation), we're automatically for God's grace. We have nothing to do with the provision of grace; it is purely the gift of God given at His discretion.

It is not because we read our bible, pray, or keep the Ten Commandments. It is not even because of our good works that we receive God's grace, but it is simply because we are His children.

The greatest help available to anyone is this grace and it is what sets us apart. Grace puts you in front and not behind. Grace makes provision for speed and success according to God's process for your life to take shape. With grace in your life, obstacles and limitations are easy to overcome. The grace of God is inexhaustible, and it covers all areas of our needs; nothing more can be added to it.

God's repertoire of grace cannot be overdrawn because the deposit is limitless. The throne of grace is always accessible to God's children; no barriers or limitations. There, we have access to anything we need to live and make it to our destiny.

The writer of Hebrews 4:16 KJV says, *"Let us therefore come boldly unto the throne of grace that we may obtain mercy, and find grace to help in time of need."*

Boldly! This boldness is not about our ability, but about what grace has made available to us. At the throne of grace, we are granted mercy that erases the punishment we deserve and strength to handle the pains we face. Grace is available to handle everything life may throw at us because God will always fulfill His promises. We must not relent in coming before the throne of grace to request for help especially in our times of need. The onus is on us to desire and approach this throne.

PRAYER SHOTS:

1. Father, please pour your grace on my lips and bless me forever.
2. Lord, let your grace be enough for my race in this life.
3. I receive grace to terminate disgrace in my life, family, career and generation, in Jesus' name.

DAY

17

ALL THINGS WORK TOGETHER FOR GOOD

TEXT: ROMANS 8:28 NKJV

"AND WE KNOW THAT ALL THINGS WORK TOGETHER FOR GOOD TO THOSE WHO LOVE GOD, TO THOSE WHO ARE THE CALLED ACCORDING TO HIS PURPOSE."

KEY NUGGET: **God will never do something great in your life without first giving you a glimpse of it!**

After leaving my home country of Nigeria in 1994 for Swaziland, I was able to secure a lucrative *locum tenens* job in a paper company and that was within two months of my arrival in that country. Apart from a great salary, this job came with perks which included a furnished house, a maid and a car. The doctor I went to cover for had traveled on an exploratory trip to Canada with the intention of eventually relocating there, but he also had an arrangement to return to his job if his plan didn't pan out. You can guess what my prayer focus was! I prayed hard and long for hours that this physician would like Canada but, contrary to my desire, he returned about four months to continue his job.

What I didn't understand initially in this situation was that God had a plan. He used my temporary job in Swaziland to unveil Canada to me.

God doesn't do great things in our life without first giving us a glimpse! The day following my leaving the Swaziland company, I got another job in a big Mission Hospital in the country.

Even though this new job's pay was smaller, God used it to develop me spiritually and used me to impact people in the process. As a matter of fact, it was from this other job I started pastoring a church! Following this, I moved to South Africa for a while before I eventually relocated to Canada in 2001. It is important to note that I had no plans of moving to Canada when I initially left my country in 1994.

Our walk of destiny could be likened to a person preparing a pot of chicken soup. The ingredients such as tomato, pepper, onions, salt, chicken, olive oil, condiments, etc., wouldn't make sense individually before they're blended together. In fact, trying to eat each one in isolation may leave a bitter taste in the mouth, but when the soup is finally made, it tastes so good that we lick our fingers and ask for more like the proverbial Oliver Twist.

A tale was told of a king who loved hunting so much that he engaged the services of a smart hunter to train him. This hunter was fond of saying, "It's all well and good", no matter the situation.

During one of their hunting adventures, the king mishandled the gun and accidentally blew off one of his own fingers. He expected the hunter to commiserate with him, but the hunter only responded with his usual, "It's all well and good". This infuriated the king and he ordered that this hunter be locked up while he decided to go hunting alone.

One night in the jungle, the king was captured by some aliens who fed on humans. As they were preparing to kill him, these aliens discovered the deformity on his hand caused by the prior gun accident. It so happened that these alien's tradition does not permit them to feed on humans with deformities, so they let him go. The king was grateful that what he considered a deformity was what saved him and suddenly, he remembered the hunter's sayings. He quickly had the hunter released and begged for his forgiveness. The hunter in his usual manner responded with, "It's all well and good".

The finger lost to an accident ended up saving the king's life. The hunter also thanked the king for locking him up in the prison and going hunting alone because if the king had taken him along, he would have been food for the aliens instead because he has no physical deformity.

The first principle in our narrative is to know that all things work together for our good. God does all things in accordance with His will in fulfilling His purpose for our lives. We may not like His methods, but He knows how to make the products fit His sovereign intentions. For instance, who would have thought that selling Joseph into slavery would align with Joseph's dreams? Who would have known that having Jonah in the belly of a fish for three days has a prophetic insinuation that would later play out in the earthly mission of Jesus Christ? Who would have imagined that the widowhood of Ruth's would be her access into the lineage of the Messiah? Paul captured it accurately in one of his epistles:

"BUT I WOULD YE SHOULD UNDERSTAND, BRETHREN, THAT THE THINGS WHICH HAPPENED UNTO ME HAVE FALLEN OUT RATHER UNTO THE FURTHERANCE OF THE GOSPEL; SO THAT MY BONDS IN CHRIST ARE MANIFEST IN ALL THE PALACE, AND IN ALL OTHER PLACES; AND MANY OF THE BRETHREN IN THE LORD, WAXING CONFIDENT BY MY BONDS, ARE MUCH MORE BOLD TO SPEAK THE WORD WITHOUT FEAR" (PHILIPPIANS 1:12-14 KJV).

There is a way that some of the challenges we face ultimately result in promoting the gospel of Jesus. There are accompanying testimonies that underscore the efficacy of the gospel in the lives of others. Apostle Paul's bonds were the links that God used to take him to the palace and areas where he was able to plant the seeds of the gospel. His bonds also encouraged and emboldened the brethren to preach the Word of God without fear. What a testimony!

If you survive your current challenges without compromise, can you imagine the number of people whose hope will be rekindled, and minds inspired? Can you imagine the distance your voice will go in announcing the manifold grace of God?

Please know for certain that the failures, errors, success, delays, accusations, criticisms, etc. you may have or may be going through, will all work together for your good, provided you love God and are committed to His call upon your life.

Prayer Shots:

1. Father, perfect that which concerns me.
2. Lord, order my steps.
3. Lord, help me to trust you with every little detail of my life.

DAY

18

DON'T LOSE HOPE

TEXT: HEBREWS 10:35 NKJV

"Therefore do not cast away your confidence, which has great reward."

KEY NUGGET: **Always have a firm grip on hope as the only way to cope.**

A piece of information I recently received destabilized me for a few hours. The effect this news on my body and soul gave me a new perspective on life. The news was so negative that it sent strong shock waves through my spine and almost sucked the air out of me. My bones felt broken, my muscles became stiff and my mouth felt heavy as tears streamed down my eyes. I was so weak that all I could do was to go climb on my bed and lie down. This episode lasted for hours until I suddenly realized that I was just about to lose hope and give up. It is indeed true that if a man loses hope, he has come to the end of his life!

Thank God for a believing partner who saw my agony and encouraged me in the Lord. I decided to fight for my life, putting my hope in God and committing to a deeper walk with Him. It is easy to tell people who are going through challenges to be strong when we don't really understand what they're going through. It is a good idea for us to seek professional help when necessary however, as believers, we need to develop a lifestyle of praise and prayer to maintain our faith in the Lord. Also, the importance of family support, godly relationships and remembering what the Lord has done in the past, cannot be overemphasized in such times.

My unpleasant experience helped me to identify with David in Psalm 42:5 KJV, *"Why art thou cast down, O my soul? and why art thou disquieted in me? hope thou in God: for I shall yet praise him for the help of his countenance."*

There are many "WHYs" in a man's life that can dampen his soul with reasons that cannot be traced to a fault of yours or any reasonable cause. Sometimes you wake up with a depressive and gloomy outlook of the future as if the whole world has lost meaning. It could get so bad when you're faced with a barrage of questions without a single answer. There are certain issues within a man's soul that cannot be expressed in words. Describing issues to people in such situations is often challenging. There are certain conversations in life that you can only have with yourself. Some inner questions though unuttered are so loud that the soul loses its serenity.

I remembered several years ago in high school when I had to sit for a university entrance examination; I found myself skipping quite a number of the questions because I had no idea what the answers were. I became anxious at a point when I realized that I had more questions left to be answered than the time I had left. Consequently, I began to make mistakes in answering the ones I thought I knew as a result. The pressure was so much that I started having a headache in the examination hall and tears began to roll down my cheeks. I was grateful to God that this test was what we termed a "mock exam"; otherwise I would have lost the opportunity to gain admission into a higher institution if it were the real deal. Before the actual examination date, I refocused my energy, elevated my resolve and exposed myself to all kinds of test questions until I could confidently face my examination phobia.

Hope gets us across life's walls of despondency; not just any hope but hope in God. Many people's hopes have been dashed despite the assurances given to them by the ones they had placed their hopes in. Some hope they will find joy in marriage contracted by law only to find out that a peaceful home cannot be achieved through legalization. A spouse may not break that law but can still break your heart. There are poor people who hoped that making more money will give them more meaning in life only to end up with more questions in their souls with bank deposit they make. Some placed hope in their parents for a guaranteed future only for death to abort their plans by snatching these parents from them.

Friends, please put your hope in God alone and make His Word a daily instructor of your soul. God is the only one that cannot disappoint you; He cannot be faced with or overcome by any adversity we humans face. No matter how solid a man's strategy of hope may look, it can fail easily in the face of adversity. Only God can be trusted; He has never failed those who trust in Him.

"They that trust in the Lord shall be as mount Zion, which cannot be removed, but abideth for ever" (Psalm 125:1 KJV).

If you trust in the Lord, you cannot be removed from the center of His plan and purpose for your life despite the storms that may face you. You may be shaken or shocked, but you won't be removed. Even when it becomes humanly impossible to hold on to God; just trust in Him and He will, in turn, hold on to you.

We must learn to put our hope in God because He is the author of our lives. He knows how to fix or replace whatever is broken (or missing) in us.

"LET YOUR CONVERSATION BE WITHOUT COVETOUSNESS; AND BE CONTENT WITH SUCH THINGS AS YE HAVE: FOR HE HATH SAID, I WILL NEVER LEAVE THEE, NOR FORSAKE THEE. SO THAT WE MAY BOLDLY SAY, THE LORD IS MY HELPER, AND I WILL NOT FEAR WHAT MAN SHALL DO UNTO ME" (HEBREWS 13:5-6 KJV).

PRAYER SHOTS:

1. Father, please help me to trust you more and more.
2. Lord, I ask that you please be my sure hope.
3. I reject hopelessness. I am born to shine. I am a victor and not a victim. I am an eagle and not a chicken.

DAY

YOU NEED A MORDECAI

TEXT: ESTHER 2:7 NKJV

"And Mordecai had brought up Hadassah, that is, Esther, his uncle's daughter, 'for she had neither father nor mother. The young woman was lovely and beautiful. When her father and mother died, Mordecai took her as his own daughter."

KEY NUGGET: **Link up with your Mordecai, your God ordained destiny helper.**

A Mordecai is someone that fulfills several roles in your life's journey. He or she could play the role of a mentor, a parent, a destiny helper, a counselor, a teacher, an instructor, a coach, etc. as you navigate through your Christian journey. They're there to ensure that you live your life to the fullest, to remain relevant, and to make it to your destination in God.

According to the Scriptures, Mordecai was Esther's uncle who also happened to be one of the servants in King Ahasuerus kingdom. He trained and brought Esther up from a tender age as his own daughter and practically nurtured her into becoming the king's wife.

When King Ahasuerus decided to replace Queen Vashti, he gathered several maidens into Shushan, the palace. Mordecai encouraged Esther to participate even though she would not have qualified because she was a Jewish captive in the land. Mordecai simply instructed her not to give out her identity. So, *"Esther had not shown her people nor her kindred: for Mordecai had charged her that she should not show it."* (Esther 2:10 KJ21).

In a visual world where little or no value is placed on the invisible and much a lot is invested on the visible, Esther must've learned as a young lady to discipline her tongue from revealing what was meant to be kept secret. Many destinies never matured into greatness because of premature exposures to influences that attracted threats and distractions. God has inputted His wisdom for living into different people and positioned them for our benefit. All we need to do is tap from their wealth of insight for our benefit.

It is funny how some people wasted their chances at greatness by refusing divine instructions. A substantial number of our young people today would only obey instructions that pander to their own emotional needs, otherwise, they will protest in rebellion. Esther needed an uncle like Mordecai who would properly train and prepare her for her great future.

There are people today living a wild and ungodly life because they refused to accept the training of the people God positioned in their lives to help cultivate them. A wild lifestyle is generally defined as a life without control or caution. You can identify well-trained people by the way they talk, dress, and relate with others. Esther was taken in at a tender age and raised by Mordecai as his own daughter.

A great influencer like Mordecai would not take someone under their arms to use for selfish reasons. Destiny helpers usually take the people they're helping as a precious and personal irrespective of their shortcomings. They, in fact, would go out of their way to cover up for such people's inadequacies.

Mordecai went out of his way to monitor Esther's progress in the court of the women where the virgins were kept. Esther was selected and eventually became the new queen.

A Mordecai would neither compete with you nor seek to wear you out; his (or her) goal is to propel you into action. A Mordecai will inspire you to take steps in the right direction. When you are discouraged and feeling down, when it seems like all your efforts are not producing the desired results, your Mordecai will motivate you. Real leaders often need someone to tell them the truth when they're not living up to expectation. When Esther was reluctant to approach the King for the deliverance of the Jews from Haman's plot, Mordecai's response was to her was, *"Do not think in your heart that you will escape in the king's palace any more than all the other Jews. For if you remain completely silent at this time, relief and deliverance will arise for the Jews from another place, but you and your father's house will perish. Yet who knows whether you have come to the kingdom for such a time as this?"* (Esther 4:13-14 NKJV).

The likes of Mordecai offer counsels based on their own life's experiences to help you believe in your ability or, if necessary, change your strategy. Remember, to constantly grow and improve your skills and life, you'll need tutors and mentors as you will benefit greatly from the insights, wisdom and experiences. Pray that God connects you to a Mordecai today if you don't have one in your life. While it is true that the Holy Spirit teaches us all things, but God still wants His people to live accountably in the community of saints and, therefore, sets the desolate in families.

PRAYER SHOTS:

1. Father, please send me a mentor that will stand beside me and not behind or above me.
2. Lord, give me men that will help me climb on their shoulders to reach my goals.
3. I humble myself to learn, obey, love, and take corrections from every Mordecai God has lined up on the path to my destiny.

NO ILLEGITIMATE CHILD

TEXT: 2 SAMUEL 12:24 NKJV

"Then David comforted Bathsheba his wife, and went in to her and lay with her. So she bore a son, and he called his name Solomon. Now the Lord loved him."

KEY NUGGET: Get rid of the illegitimacy label in your life

With the rising level of illegitimate relationships in the 21st century, one wonders how the children born from the various circumstances would be viewed. A lot of children are born to different parents today using different methods, especially through assisted reproduction. For example, surrogacy is gaining ground among infertile or gay couples. It is important to note, however, that every child born into this world has a destiny from heaven. I believe no one should be defined by the circumstances surrounding their birth. As a child of God, you are unique, and thus a winner from your conception.

This is because millions of spermatozoa competed for one egg during your conception and you happened to be the winning one. Know for sure that God has a purpose and special plans for your life. Jesus died for the sins of every human being on this earth. As a result, anybody who accepts

Him as personal Saviour gains access to all the accompanying benefits without restrictions to the height you can attain in the Lord. So, get rid of all illegitimacy labels that could hold you back in life! Don't allow the devil to capitalize on that and use them to torment you with what you cannot control.

Solomon was a product of the union between David and Bathsheba, the wife of the late Uriah whom David had killed after their initial illegitimate relationship. After Uriah's death, David proceeded to marry Bathsheba and Solomon was the eventual outcome of their marriage. Solomon later ascended the throne of his father, David. King Solomon became the wisest person to live on earth until the arrival of our Lord Jesus Christ on earth. Despite the circumstances surrounding Solomon's birth, he was able to surmount his challenges and became one of the greatest kings Israel ever had. You too can rise above any obstacle life may bring your way!

One may wonder how God could love the product of such an immoral background. God did not endorse the circumstances that led to Solomon's birth. As a matter of fact, He frowned at it and ensured David suffered the attending consequences. Solomon was still God's creation who, in his own right, won the heart of God regardless of his background. We are not who our place of origin made us; rather, we are who God defines us to be.

Uriah's family may dislike Solomon; his enemies may not have looked favourably on him. In short, many people who knew his history would not want their children relating with him; this, however, never affected God's love for him and that's all that matters. Glory to God! His divine endorsement and His love for you is all that counts.

No amount of hatred can quench the love of the Father for you. We erroneously seek people's affection to eradicate the fault lines on our identities, but we end up getting shattered when such people withdraw their emotional support or fail to live up to expectations. Our fault lines could hereditary or due to our past mistakes.

Many people committed suicide because they felt unloved by people who were privy to their terrible past. We must understand that every saint has a sinful past and that every sinner can attain a sinless future. You must never allow anything, or anyone separate you from the love of God in Christ Jesus. Don't let your ugly past hinder your bright future. The word of God assures us that Jesus Christ cleared the errors of our past by,

"Blotting out the handwriting of ordinances that was against us, which was contrary to us, and took it out of the way, nailing it to the cross" (Colossians 2:14 KJV). Here we are assured that no ordinance is strong enough to slow down or stop the advancement of a true believer in Christ Jesus.

It is sheer ignorance for Christians to assume that certain ancestral curses are still active in their lives. By the single act of the Lord Jesus on the cross, every curse that is contrary to you has been blotted out. The only ordinances permitted to operate in your life are those in line with the will of God for you.

God's children are no longer under the law of sin and death, but under the Lord of the Spirit of life in Christ Jesus. Therefore, whenever the devil reminds you of your erased past, give him a reminder of his doomed future in the bottomless pit.

This amazing reality is further affirmed by Paul, the Apostle in Ephesians 1:6 KJV thus, *"To the praise of the glory of his grace, wherein he hath made us accepted in the beloved."*

We are not invited into God's beloved for sightseeing; no, we have been accepted and fully adopted by our heavenly Father without any further qualifications such as education, self-righteousness, social background verification, or subscription fee is required. We are accepted in the beloved simply by his grace. Friend, it doesn't matter what your disadvantaged history has cost you; you have already been accepted where it matters most.

PRAYER SHOTS:

1. Father, please remove every evil label that men have placed on me.
2. Lord, grant me a new beginning in victory, breakthrough, joy, peace and success.
3. I receive the power to set my life in motion and move forward, in Jesus' name.

DAY

21

DO NOT ENVY

TEXT: GENESIS 37:3-4 NKJV

"Now Israel loved Joseph more than all his children, because he was the son of his old age. Also he made him a tunic of many colors. But when his brothers saw that their father loved him more than all his brothers, they hated him and could not speak peaceably to him."

KEY NUGGET: **The grass was fine until it looked greener on the other side; those who compare themselves with others are never wise.**

Jacob served under hard labour for fourteen years just to marry Rachel, his heartthrob. Unfortunately, Rachel was barren for many years until she eventually gave Jacob a son in Jacob's old age named Joseph. Obviously, the birth of Joseph came at a painful cost to Jacob who went through so much heartache before his eventual conception.

Joseph was born after Jacob's youthful strengths and abilities were already waning. The circumstances surrounding Joseph's birth made him a victim of conflicts and contradictions. The fact that he was born by Rachel, the woman that Jacob loved, made Joseph enjoyed special privileges as his father's favorite son. This, of course, attracted the envy and hatred of his brothers. Sometimes, your colourful and beautiful life could be the source of your battles. It is difficult to thrive spiritually when your father's love for you is greeted by the hatred of your very own siblings.

It is amazing that people are quick to hate the very ones whom God, the Father, loves. If the hatred and envy Joseph experienced had come from strangers, it would have been understandable, but the hatred came from within his household.

They started envying him when they saw their father's increased love for him. In the same vein, God's love for us is so visible that it naturally attracts negative reactions from those who felt bypassed by Him to give you what they deserved. Some people believe they are more deserving of God's attention that you are. The moment the love of God becomes visible on your ministry, your marriage and even your business, begin to expect oppositions of envy and hatred from people, especially the brethren!

Some folks simply can't stand by and watch you enjoy the love of God. Joseph's father made him a multicoloured tunic and this further provoked his brothers to jealousy. Beware, because the things God is preparing for you will also attract the envy of others! The uniqueness of the kind of honour the Father bestowed on you may be too colourful for some people to tolerate. Don't think your being hated is due to your character flaws; rather consider the fact that it may be because of the tunic of grace and glamour that God is making for you.

Envy is can be defined as the feeling of displeasure the sight or news of an advantage someone has over you. The synonyms of envy are jealousy, rivalry, resentment, and bitterness. Envy such an evil that is rampant in the 21st century due to the competitive nature of our world today. Everyone is striving to best the rest, and many are unwilling to, either wait for their time, or put in the necessary effort for success. Envy has driven some to do the unthinkable. The first recorded murder in the Bible was as a result of envy. Cain was envious of the fact that God accepted his brother, Abel's offering while his was rejected and this was enough to make him murder his very own blood brother.

Envy is also a psychological admission of inferiority to the object of one's envy. It is an evidence of inadequacy ravaging the thoughts of its victim. Those who envy others are not interested in knowing why the people they envy are so loved by the Father. Joseph's brother failed to consider the fact that he was carrying out a godly service by bringing reports of their wayward acts to their father. All they cared about was that he got more attention than they did, and they hated him for that.

The spirit of envy competes with others with the intention to slander the other person and therefore outshine them. Such a spirit will hate to pay the price that gives the envied person the advantage but would desire to have even more than the person has. It's easy to slide into envy when your commitment to personal development and spiritual growth is gone.

We can, however, overcome envy by looking unto Jesus and being content with what we have and who we are in the Him. Sometimes, it is necessary for you to know and understand the story behind the glory of those you perceived as having an advantage over you. The popular saying, "If you want my gains be ready to carry my pains" is very true. The truth is a lot happens behind the scenes of many people's lives, but we're only exposed to the façade most of the time.

PRAYER SHOTS:

Father, please give me a winning mindset.
Lord, give me a contented heart.
I receive an overcomer's mentality in Jesus' name.

DAY

22

BE ROYAL

TEXT: 1 PETER 2:9 NKJV

"But you are a chosen generation, a royal priesthood, a holy nation, His own special people, that you may proclaim the praises of Him who called you out of darkness into His marvelous light."

KEY NUGGET: You will be addressed the way you are dressed!

Identity crisis seems to be the toughest conflict facing many people today. Until people can catch a revelation of their identity, they will always tend to misbehave. The consciousness of who we are will keep us from certain places, from doing certain things and from mixing with certain people. The first clue to our identity is that we're God's chosen generation. There are several generations of people on this earth yet not all are God's choice. His preference for us can also be seen through our identity. God doesn't just choose people and leave them the way they are; He also trains and empowers them with what they need to become more like Him.

When a king chooses someone to sit with him, such a person's life is upgraded and granted access to royal benefits. There are people who live poor and subdued lives because they are ignorant of their value to

God. This could probably explain why some women find themselves in relationships with guys with little or no regard for their dignity. Such women are ignorant of their divine position in Christ.

When some people experience broken relationships, they lose the grip on their spiritual lives because they had assumed that having a spouse is what will validate them socially. The day you become aware that you're God's premium choice, your attitude towards rejection by men will be different.

The fact that you are God's own automatically imparts royalty and priesthood on you. Every true believer in Christ Jesus occupies a very strategic position of grace, kingship and priesthood. As God's children, we reign in righteousness; representing God in the sight of men and interceding for men before God. We are not just relevant in the worship assemblies; we are also significant in decision-making palaces. Our uniqueness as God's chosen enables us to function with eternal relevance in a temporal world.

The crown of our dignity is the fact that we're made partakers of the divine nature. We're a nation of holy people representing our divine tribe here on earth. This is the watermark of distinction embedded in our spiritual passports. We don't live ungodly lives, think dirty thoughts or engage in filthy deals. Whatever our godly minds cannot digest would not be found in our mouths. We raise pure families, run pure businesses, oversee pure ministries, speak pure languages, live in purity and exercise ourselves unto godliness and because our spirits are allergic to sin, we don't feel comfortable in it.

We are a very special breed of people called to fulfil God's desired purpose for us through Christ Jesus. We are not special because of the cars we drive or the mansions we live in; we are special because everything we do brings praises to the Lord. When people meet us, they glorify God for causing our paths to cross. When we enter an organization, our election and priesthood cause things to turn around for the good of such an establishment. Moribund companies begin to make profits and depressed associates receive hope and discouraged acquaintances press forward with renewed strength.

I happen to come from a royal family and have been privileged to keenly observe the way they conduct themselves. They are trained to pay attention to details to prevent bringing the crown to a state of disrepute.

We also must learn to demonstrate royalty in our appearances. A king does not appear unkempt before his subjects. He must always look good and majestic. You too must endeavor to always display the appropriate image for your surroundings. Let your dressing be modest, however, as you will be addressed by the way you dress. Be aware that your appearance creates an impression and it is often very tough to overcome a poor first impression.

Be noble with your words too. Don't be crude or rude; avoid profane jokes as people are more likely to take your words seriously. Words are so powerful that they can make or break you, therefore, let your words be seasoned with grace. Your words should not be cheap and careless either. Let your words be your bond. Don't promise (or commit to) what you cannot do. Don't be negative or abusive. Remember that a king's words contain power as aptly captured in Ecclesiastes 8:4 NKJV, *"Where the word of a king is, there is* power; *And who may say to him, "What are you doing?"*

Be regal in your emotional expressions. Learn to control your temper. Don't give in to any pressure. Be quick to listen, slow to speak and slow to anger. Proverbs 16:32 WEB says, *"One who is slow to anger is better than the mighty; one who rules his spirit than he who takes a city."*

Do not let your emotions get the better of you.

Lastly, be kingly in your thoughts and actions. Put excellence into everything you do. Do not seek shortcuts rather, show high moral standards in your work. Don't settle for anything less than the best. As the saying goes, "Whatever is worth doing at all is worth doing well". Be known for excellence! Don't break the rules!

PRAYER SHOTS:

1. Father, please clothe me with royalty, beauty and dignity.
2. I declare that I am God's special person.
3. This day, I receive by faith the kind of blessings money cannot buy from God.

DAY

BE FRUGAL

TEXT: JOHN 6:12 NKJV

SO WHEN THEY WERE FILLED, HE SAID TO HIS DISCIPLES,
"GATHER UP THE FRAGMENTS THAT REMAIN, SO THAT
NOTHING IS LOST."

KEY NUGGET: **You can be frugal without cramping your style; it's the wise thing to do!**

We must learn to move from waste to wealth. A great deal of what people waste today could be converted to future investments. Some people waste food in their homes without any remorse or thought of those who would do anything to get a taste of what they considered trash. One of the rules that should be established in our Christian homes is to responsibly preserve resources. Jesus laid out a very important principle for us in today's text. He showed us that there are times when God supplies you with more than enough to meet your needs. If He uses you as a channel of such a provision, you should also understand that your duty goes beyond the supply. You must endeavour to preserve the leftovers because what you do with the surplus is a demonstration of your frugality or lack thereof. Many people discard their leftovers once they have eaten to their satisfaction.

Waste is a display of carnality; an act of disobedience to the counsel of prudence. We can infer that our Lord's instruction to the disciples to gather the fragments is also applicable to us today for our admonition. Jesus is teaching us here to be accountable even for fragments which we might consider insignificant. Nothing must be lost! The question then is how much of our wasted resources are we able to account for at the end of the day?

Some Christians even find it offensive when asked to account for resources committed to their care. We have couples who fight over accountability issues because certain expenditures cannot be accounted for. Are you able to account for how much you may have lost since you started earning an income? Is the money entrusted to your care by your spouse intact? Can you give a proper account of the resources your department at work placed under your watch?

The duty of a true disciple of Jesus Christ is to first meet people's needs and afterwards gather the fragments. The evidence that you have done the job faithfully is that nothing is lost! It is always important to remind ourselves that we are stewards of God's resources here on earth. You should not be spending your resources careless without making plans to save for the future. Learn how to be contented with whatever you have.

You should know that life is in stages and seasons. There are seasons of scarcity as well as seasons of abundance. So, get into the habit of saving for the rainy day. Check how you spend your money and block any loopholes that you may discover. Proverbs 22:3 NIV says, *"The prudent see danger and take refuge, but the simple keep going and pay the penalty."*

Many times, we waste resources because we are oblivious of future needs. Joseph's counsel to the Pharaoh for the preservation of Egypt's national economy was to store away resources in the years of plenty in order to sustain the people in the years of scarcity. We should take a cue from Joseph and cultivate a saving and wise investment mentality for the future instead of going on a careless spending spree that comes with devastating consequences.

Remember that, at least, ten percent of your earnings belong to God so don't try to rob God (see Malachi 3:8-10 KJV). In the same vein, you should also endeavour to save a minimum of ten percent of your earnings. Do not be guided by your emotions because it is likely to fool you. Try not to be desperate. Take some time to sleep over your choices before deciding. That way, you'll be positioned to make the right choice.

Stop buying what you don't need. Don't spend the money you don't have to impress people who don't know you. Watch out especially for the *"buy it now and pay later"* sales gimmicks! Spending money to make social statements is not a sign of wisdom. Always avoid the debt trap on consumption.

The wisest person who ever lived said in Proverbs 22:7 NKJV, *"The rich rules over the poor, and the borrower is servant to the lender."*

The world is framed in such a manner that rulership is reserved for the rich and those who lend are masters to borrowers. In a status driven economy, one must be wise to avoid being wrongly positioned due to poor financial decisions. Little can become so much when the flow of resources is rooted in accountability. Lastly, always set your yearly financial goals. Be diligent, have a financial mentor and be determined to succeed in life. Remember, no one can manage your finances better than you.

PRAYER SHOTS:

1. Dear Father in heaven, please increase me in wisdom.
2. Dear God, let me be dignified, promoted and enjoy greatness in life.
3. I declare that I am a prudent manager of God's resources in my life in Jesus' name.

DAY

BE ROOTED AND BUILT UP

TEXT: COLOSSIANS 2:7 NKJV

"ROOTED AND BUILT UP IN HIM, AND ESTABLISHED IN
THE FAITH, AS YOU HAVE BEEN TAUGHT, ABOUNDING IN
IT WITH THANKSGIVING."

KEY NUGGET: **Stay rooted and grounded in your faith in Christ
because if you stand for nothing, you will fall for
anything.**

The part of a plant's embryo that develops into the primary root is
called the radicle. It is the first part of a seedling to emerge from the seed
during the process of germination. The stability of the plant from the
tender stage to the mature phase is anchored on the strength of its root. If
issues arise while the radicle is developing, the plant will break or bow to
the beatings of the wind. Even so, the stability of every man is anchored
in his foundational root.

The greatest threat to the faith of a believer in our modern world is
when the Word of God—the foundation on which our faith is built—
is being threatened by apostasy and false doctrines. The emergence of
modern believers who lack roots in the basic tenets of faith is threatening
the voice of truth in the hearts of these shallow Christians. Therefore,

many of them cannot withstand trials and persecution because their faith that cannot survive adversity. They feed largely on the milk of God's word and scarcely imbibe anything spiritual during church service. They can spend millions of dollars going to musical concerts and stay up all night at jamborees but will hardly stay awake listening to God's Word.

This probably explains why some ministers (and ministries) are investing more energy and resources in promoting religious activities at the expense of their relationship with Jesus and studying the Word. They buy their way up the ladder of church leadership through compromise, eye service and bribery, but they are stunted in their spiritual growth. When you listen to some of these celebrity ministers (some of who oversee well-established Christian organizations), you would be heartbroken for the mess they call messages.

Only those rooted and built up in Christ can withstand trying times. When expectations are disappointed, those who have survived the wilderness of trials would be the ones standing (those rooted and built up in Him), not the ones with a status symbol. A plant cannot be rooted where it is not planted. Many ministers today are more rooted in secular life than the spiritual. They are more inclined towards politics and power than an encounter with the person of Jesus.

Teaching is critical to the foundation, building and establishment of a true Christian's faith. How a man is taught determines how he, in turn, teaches others. Many people are taught the theory of Christianity without practical examples from those who taught them. They are familiar with Biblical requirements for leadership, marriage, business, ministries, etc., but they have no clear examples to validate the truth.

The 21st century is a toxic environment. Technology, as good as it is, has made living a godly life also very difficult. Christians are losing their identities at a fast pace because the world has been so polluted, and the gospel so watered down that what was once evil a few years ago is now acceptable. I also discovered, to my amazement, that words that were considered vulgar a few decades back are now common parlance, even on national television.

Peer pressure has caused some people to lose their identity in Christ. The decisions of many lives are influenced by constant pressure from their peers because it's not easy for them to be the odd one out.

Daniel one of the slaves carried away to Babylon where the king had prescribed a special diet for the captive boys to prepare them for serving in his palace. Though in captivity, Daniel refused to compromise his identity by rejecting the pressure of living an ungodly lifestyle in a strange land. In Daniel 1:8 NIV we read, *"But Daniel resolved not to defile himself with the royal food and wine, and he asked the chief official for permission not to defile himself this way"*.

Most of the perks offered by some organizations to prospective employees today are often contaminating to their faith in Christ. True Christians must, therefore, intentionally resolve not to be defiled by these enticing offers at the expense of their faith. Daniel was so rooted in his faith in God that no food and wine could uproot him. It's sad and shocking to see how people are easily uprooted from their faith by worldly incentives today. They give in to mundane things such as alluring relationships, compromising employment opportunities, ungodly business contracts, travel visa assistance, and so on, simply because of the pressure to get ahead in life.

Another reason why many lose their identities is the fear of man. Many are afraid to confront situations that threaten their beliefs. We must be ready to fight for our identities in the face of intimidations and threats from the world. The three Hebrew boys: Shadrach, Meshach and Abednego, stood up for their faith and refused to serve a false god or worship Nebuchadnezzar's golden image, even at the peril of death by a fiery furnace (see Daniel 3:13-15 NKJV).

Nebuchadnezzar threatened them in his fierce anger, but they refused to be intimidated and answered the king by saying, *"King Nebuchadnezzar, we do not need to defend ourselves before you in this matter. If we are thrown into the blazing furnace, the God we serve is able to deliver us from it, and he will deliver us from Your Majesty's hand. But even if he does not, we want you to know, Your Majesty, that we will not serve your gods or worship the image of gold you have set up"* (Daniel 3:16-18, NIV).

You too can maintain your identity in this dark world by staying resolute in your faith, keeping godly association and, staying connected and rooted in the Lord Jesus.

PRAYER SHOTS:

1. Father, I pray that you make my hands clean and increase my strength. Let me be stronger and stronger as the days go by.
2. Lord, deliver me from the jaws of lions on the road to my destiny.
3. I declare that I am a holy nation called forth to sing God's praises.

DAY

25

REDEEM THE TIME

TEXT: EPHESIANS 5:15-16 NKJV

"See then that you walk circumspectly, not as fools but as wise, redeeming the time, because the days are evil."

KEY NUGGET: **Take full advantage of every day and commit your life to His purpose**

Time is universal; everyone has twenty-four hours in a day—whether you are young or old, poor or rich, busy or idle. What we do in the space of time does not end now but flows into and influences our future. A popular African proverb says, "A young man who runs from labour under the sun will spend his night naked in the cold". We must make hay while the sun shines. Procrastination is the thief of time and today's duties must be attended to now because tomorrow's success is dependent on them. A wise once man said that whenever God intends to do something important, He engages the services of busy and productive people.

In today's Bible text, the first way to maximize time is to reflect on how we live our lives from one point in time to another. Our daily walk must be reviewed—and revised where necessary—on a constant basis. We should not spend our time without a holistic audit of what and who give our time to and consider the attending consequences of such investments. If we are not deliberate about how we spend our time we will end up wasting it.

We are admonished in our text to walk circumspectly; that is, to walk with a well-rounded awareness. Many times, we venture into time-wasting ventures and life-ruining relationships because we only view things from just one angle. Thus, we are limited in understanding due to myopic vision or partial information. Many accidents on the highway could be avoidable if most of the drivers would check first before speeding into a busy intersection. One can distinguish between a fool and a wise man simply by the way they make decisions. The devil knows how to blind us from reflecting on the consequences of our actions before making decisions. We must learn to verify things from reliable sources before taking steps that may alter the equilibrium of our lives.

Time is like a vapor that evaporates quietly but consistently; you may not even notice it until your hair begins to turn gray and your children who were once toddlers now trim their beards at the same saloon with you. The way to maximize time is to containerize it in a cylinder of wisdom for a determined purpose. We must be intentionally accountable for every minute we have to live. Ask yourself, "What have I set out to do this year, this month, this week, even today?" Where time is not associated with purpose, life would be a waste.

We can also redeem time through collaboration with others by leveraging their strength and capacity to mutually accomplish what is impossible by an individual. There is a multiplying effect in synergizing which confirms that two are better than one because they're able to achieve better rewards for their unified efforts. Many people waste their time because they find it difficult to work on a team that could've amplified their productive capacity. They'll rather operate in isolation hoping to impress others with the result of their solo efforts only to realize they've wasted precious time accomplishing nothing.

Most productive people in the world work in teams, lending their expertise towards a common goal. They work interdependently to achieve the greater good for everyone's benefit. One of the reasons many can't fit into a team environment is because they are ignorant and selfish when it comes to working with others towards a common goal. Some rich folks have lost competent and trustworthy servants because they have zero appreciation for their services. Such employees abandon their ungrateful bosses to work for those who value them. Some poor people are unable to redeem their time because they lack the fortitude to positively impact the progress of their employer's ventures, but only seek to get rich quickly at their expense.

As alluded to earlier, time is life so, to waste your time is tantamount to wasting your life. That is why it is crucial to always redeem the time. One of the ways to master the art of productive time use is to be punctual with our responsibilities. Time is also likened to currency hence to waste it is to issue an open invitation to poverty. We must challenge ourselves to work at redeeming the time because the days we live in are few and evil.

Life is too short to lose focus. Work at making a great and significant impact on your generation. Don't waste your time on unproductive activities and the unfruitful pursuits of darkness.

Pay attention to your health by eating right and exercising regularly. Sitting related diseases are common in the 21st century because a lot of people sit more than they walk or stand. Little wonder then why they are slow, weak and dull nowadays. You need a balanced diet and regular exercise to be fit, healthy, strong and smart.

Highlight all the distractions in your life. Identify time thieves by analyzing how you spend every hour, minute and second of your day. Avoid frivolities and distractions such as gossip, quarrels, ungodly relationships, television, social media, etc.

Lastly, make full use of your time. Take advantage of any spare time you may have and do something meaningful with it. For instance, when I am on a long flight, I do a lot of reading and writing, and this has helped me to be much more productive.

In order to make our life count and be able to redeem lost time, we need to involve God in our life's schedules.

PRAYER SHOT:

Father, please deliver me from time wasters and wasters of energy.

Lord, Please Release All My Blessings From All The Four Corners Of The World To Me.

I declare that it's my time for miracles and my season of breakthroughs.

DAY

FAST AND PRAY

TEXT: MATTHEW 6:16-18 TPT

"When you fast, don't look like those who pretend to be spiritual. They want everyone to know they're fasting, so they appear in public looking miserable, gloomy, and disheveled. Believe me, they've already received their reward in full. When you fast, don't let it be obvious, but instead, wash your face and groom yourself, and realize that your Father in the secret place is the one who is watching all that you do in secret and will continue to reward you openly."

KEY NUGGET: **Fasting helps us focus, make us fit, firm and faster than our enemies.**

Fasting and praying should never be relegated to the back of our Christian journey. Jesus said, "When you fast", not "If you fast". This means that we are expected to fast from time to time. Also, God wants us to voluntarily choose when we want to fast. Many Christians do not have set times for fasting throughout the year. They have no schedule of "when to fast" on their life's calendar until tragedy strikes or they lose their appetite.

Jesus gave us certain principles to help make fasting productive in our lives and he began with what not to do. Fasting must be done as a personal thing between you and the Lord and not to flaunt our spiritual profile on social media or in the neighbourhood. Some people fast so they can be seen publicly as being spiritual and prayerful. Sadly, such people's fast is nothing but a hunger strike. The only person who needs to know you are really fasting is the Lord; no one else. When you fast to advertise your prayer commitment, you already have your reward from God. Publicity does not validate your spirituality.

A true fast is one done without public display. The kind of publicity some Christians give to fasting has already invalidated the exercise. Don't wear your fast on your countenance. Endeavour to always look presentable, more importantly, during your period of fasting. Your goal is to draw God's attention— not seek to be noticed by people—so you don't miss your full reward. An open advertisement of fasting denies you of your private reward from God.

The secret place is the place where God notices and rewards those who fast in sincerity. The number of days you fasted would be irrelevant and you also won't be rewarded if you are not willing to keeping your fast a secret between you and God.

God does not outsource the reward of fasting to a pastor or a prophet; He personally rewards those who follow His set out conditions. You may be anointed or receive impartation in the church for fasting, but this does not translate into the reward that only the Father who sees you in the secret place can give.

An incident occurred during the earthly ministry of our Lord Jesus that transformed the lives of His disciples: A man whose son was possessed by a dumb and deaf spirit could not be delivered by the disciples when the father brought him to them for deliverance. The disciples tried their utmost to set the boy free, but his condition only got worse, but when the case was brought to the attention of the Lord Jesus, the boy was instantly healed. The disciples later asked Jesus why they could not heal the boy despite their rigorous long-winded deliverance prayers while all it took was a simple rebuke of the foul spirit by the Lord for the boy to be made whole.

Jesus then revealed the secret to them in Mark 9:29 NKJV by saying, *"This kind can come out by nothing but prayer and fasting."*

Simply put, Jesus was making His disciples see the power in fasting and praying. In other words, some things that can be dealt with through sound understanding of the Scriptures and being in fellowship with God but there are others that won't yield without you fasting and praying. The potential of a non-praying Christian is subject to limitations and a lid is placed on the capacity of a believer who is only good at quoting the scriptures but a failure when it comes to prayer. You cannot suspend the requirements of fasting and prayer when confronted with demonic opposition.

Fasting is defined as abstinence from food (or pleasurable things) for some time. Fasting helps to keep our flesh in check and makes us more alert and open to hearing God. As a matter of fact, some Christians would need to do a talking or spending fast that tends towards carnality. Jesus also fasted for forty days and forty nights. Jesus was able to focus on God during this time and it is recorded in Luke 4:14 NIV that, *"Jesus returned to Galilee in the power of the Spirit, and news about him spread through the whole countryside."*

The power of the Holy Ghost found multiplied expressions in Him during the period of fasting and praying. There are returns you cannot make until you have fasted and prayed. A Christian who does not fast and pray cannot have certain exploits or a great impact.

Fasting is a price we all need to pay in order to sort ourselves out. Fasting makes us faster than our enemies. It gives us the necessary stimulus, power, strength, direction, etc., to resist the devil and frustrate his attack on our faith. The early apostles had a habit of fasting and praying before they take any major decisions.

Acts 13:2-3 NIV says, *"While they were worshiping the Lord and fasting, the Holy Spirit said, 'set apart for me Barnabas and Saul for the work to which I have called them' so after they had fasted and prayed, they placed their hands on them and sent them off."*

Paul the Apostle was highly successful in his ministry and he said the secret of his results was the fact that he fasted often (2 Corinthians 11:27 NIV). He devoted himself to fasting and praying before he could reach out to others. You too can pay the price of fasting and praying without ceasing. Remember, we need to be sorted out before we can minister to other people.

PRAYER SHOTS:

1. Father, please give me the grace to pay the price of fasting.
2. Lord, through fasting and praying, make me faster than my enemies.
3. I receive the power to discipline my body and appetite in the area of fasting and praying.

DAY

27

STOP COMPLAINING; START PRAISING

TEXT: HABAKKUK 1:2-4 NKJV

"O Lord, how long shall I cry, And You will not hear? Even cry out to You, "Violence!" And You will not save. Why do You show me iniquity, And cause me to see trouble? For plundering and violence are before me; There is strife, and contention arises. Therefore the law is powerless, And justice never goes forth. For the wicked surround the righteous; Therefore perverse judgment proceeds."

KEY NUGGET: Complaining only complicates concerns.

The name *Habakkuk* means "embracing." Habakkuk was, however, known as a complaining prophet. His complaints range from why God wasn't answering his prayers or intervening in his country's matters to why God would allow the wicked to prosper.

HOW LONG?

One of the major reasons people complain is because they believe God's response time to their emergencies is too slow. They believe that their emergencies ought to be God's emergencies too. When they cry to Him about their marital problems, careers issues or ministry challenges (and have fulfilled the religious rites prescribed by their prophets), they conclude that God is obligated to respond favourably to their righteous "acts."

Some Christians even tag their petitions "automatic prayers, automatic answers!" They believe God must respond when they want Him to. We live in a fast-food generation that lacks the patience of going through the process but are good at venting out their frustrations at God for every disappointment or delay.

They often escalate their cries to screams intending to get God to intervene in their situations and treat such as emergencies. It's like when toddlers throw tantrums so their parents can abandon whatever they're doing and focus on them.

A good example that comes to mind was a time when my younger daughter incurred the spanking of her older siblings and then screamed out so loud just to make my wife and I think something terrible had happened to her. By the time we eventually heard the whole story we discovered that the one who cried out was not the victim. So, from experience, we've learnt to sometimes allow the situation between them to play out so our younger daughter would also learn to respect her older siblings.

While God is not the author of violence, He may delay intervening if this will teach His people to obey Him and follow His commandments. It is important to understand that God loves us too much to allow the flood of life to wash us away without Him intervening. He is committed to preserving us for His purpose if we are attuned to following His instructions. So, when challenges arise and God appears slow in coming to our aid, we must continue asking for His help until He comes through for us.

For instance, God answered the prophet Habakkuk but went further to demonstrate to the prophet that His ways are not the same as our ways by using a worse sinner to punish Habakkuk's people for their sins. This goes to show us the fact that God owes no man apologies or explanations. This truth is also reiterated in Psalms 115 verse 3b NKJV where we read that "He does whatsoever He pleases." It is wise for us to understand that we are subject to God's will in this life and that He reserves the absolute right to do whatsoever He desires as our Creator.

Some of the reasons people complain include:

Faithlessness: this is when you can't see light at the end of the tunnel (Genesis 18 NKJV).

- Laziness: many don't want to work hard (Matthew 20:1-16 NKJV). They also fail to acknowledge their agreement with God (Colossians 1:26 NKJV Christ in you the hope of glory).
- Haziness: this is a like having a tunnel vision and failure to consider other possible options (2 Kings 4:28 NKJV read the account of the Shunamite woman).
- Craziness: this is when you think you deserve certain privileges, respect, and attention (Numbers 12:1-2 NKJV Mariam and Aaron).
- Hastiness: this is impatience (Exodus 32 NKJV Israelites in the wilderness).
- Lack of brokenness: this includes feelings
- of selfishness, hurt and woundedness. It is the exploitation of others and the Elder brother syndrome (Luke 15:25-32 NKJV the elder brother of the prodigal son).
- Un-thankfulness: this is ungratefulness (Jonah 4 NKJV). It is invaluable to remember that millions of people would love to trade places with you for the privileges you are ungrateful for.

The prophet Habakkuk finally resolved to acknowledge that God is his Rock, He is both holy and is in control of all things. It is important to always see God in your situation because it will help activate a lifestyle of praises and eradicate a lifestyle of complaints.

PRAYER SHOTS:

- Father, please remove every complaining spirit from me.
- Lord, please release your joyful spirit into my life.
- I will be optimistic, upbeat and enthusiastic in Jesus' name.

DAY

28

IF YOU WAIT ON GOD YOU CANNOT WASTE IN LIFE

TEXT: HABAKKUK 2:1 NKJV

"I WILL STAND MY WATCH. AND SET MYSELF ON THE RAMPART, AND WATCH TO SEE WHAT HE WILL SAY TO ME, AND WHAT I WILL ANSWER WHEN I AM CORRECTED."

KEY NUGGET: SET A STANDARD TO STAND ON UNTIL GOD SHOWS UP.

We must develop the right posture for the right spiritual adventure in Christ. Many Christians have become irrelevant because they slacked off and slept off on their watch. The sensitivity required to watch entails being on one's feet and being in a vantage position for an accurate view of possibilities. Some people are experts in monitoring the personal matters of others while ignoring their problems. We have ministers today who have spent years developing and watching over young people in their congregation, but their children rot in immorality and all forms of ungodliness.

A smart watchman is always at a vantage position to view things and adjust or make necessary corrections. Some people miss out in life simply because they are not positioned on the right rampart for a clear view of what God is revealing to them. Others, unfortunately, remain rigid in their cultural and traditional comfort zones instead of taking bold steps to climb the walls of exposure and towers of learning.

There are realities that would remain hidden until we intentionally take steps towards seeing them. Some realities travel rather too swift for the one who is distracted to see. There are moments you can only capture when your spiritual lens is positioned well ahead in anticipation. When God speaks, the words form pictures for you to properly see what He intends. God often speaks in pictures in order to help us properly understand Him. There are things God may not say to you until He's certain that you're watching with dogged focus and are poised to act.

We need to realize that waiting on God is not about wishing, asking or interceding. Rather, waiting on God is likened to a server waiting on a customer. The waiter's duty is to politely take customers' orders and serve them exactly what they want and not impose his or her preferences on them. In the same vein, we're at God's service while waiting on Him to *place His orders* at His pleasure. We are strictly at His service, keenly observing to do His bid and making Him the centre of our focus. We also seek to know Him, understand Him and glorify Him.

> "BUT THEY THAT WAIT UPON THE LORD SHALL RENEW THEIR STRENGTH; THEY SHALL MOUNT UP WITH WINGS AS EAGLES; THEY SHALL RUN, AND NOT BE WEARY; AND THEY SHALL WALK, AND NOT FAINT" (ISAIAH 40:31 KJV).

Those who hustle around in their efforts end up weaker in life, but those who wait upon the Lord become stronger. To look up to men for help will only weaken you when they eventually begin to disappoint you. Therefore, it is important to ensure that when we wait, we're waiting on God and not on men. It is only when we go this route that we can be assured of renewed strength, and the strength we gain during waiting must be invested in doing God's will and walking with Him by faith.

A strong cord is composed of strands of strings woven together. The greater the number of strings, the stronger the cord becomes. Likewise, if you can be so bound to God in patience and prayers, the resultant "rope" becomes stronger. God then becomes your strength, your shield, and every good thing imaginable.

Waiting on God also brings you renewal. Many people have run out of relevance in life because they have not learned to wait. Their past seemed to be stronger than their present. Some of these people can be identified with notable activities with little or no record of tangible productivity.

Hannah was an example of a woman who understood the power of waiting on God. She initially fought, complained and ranted about her barrenness. However, she later changed her attitude and decided to wait on God in prayers, worship and praise; she trusted God and made Him her focus (see 1 Samuel 2:1-10 NKJV). Her new approach triggered God's awesome response as recorded in 1 Samuel 2:21 NKJV: *"The Lord visited Hannah, so that she conceived and bore three sons and two daughters. Meanwhile the child Samuel grew before the Lord."*

You cannot wait on God and be ignored by Him. He will surely visit you, and that, at the right time. God would hardly visit people who are in a hurry. There are things we can only conceive through divine visitation. The capacity God gives us to carry the vision also comes with the strength to deliver it too.

A nudge from heaven is enough to set you up for a long time on earth.

PRAYER SHOTS:

1. Father, please give me a tip that will settle me for life.
2. Lord, I receive strength to wait on you.
3. I desire a sensitive heart to receive from God as I wait on Him.

DAY

BE FRUITFUL!

TEXT: GENESIS 1:28 NKJV

"Then God blessed them, and God said to them, 'Be fruitful and multiply; fill the earth and subdue it; have dominion over the fish of the sea, over the birds of the air, and over every living thing that moves on the earth.'"

KEY NUGGET: Life is meaningful only when we are fruitful.

God's blessing on every life is an investment for their fulfillment. The blessing that God blessed "them" in our text was beyond their physical blessing. It also speaks to man's innate ability to be spiritually, physically and biologically productive. For instance, God's order for sustaining the generation of His living creation is reproduction. The evidence that God expects us to be fruitful is woven into His blessing pronounced upon the first man, Adam. We can see how some people are blessed with artistic abilities, others with critical thinking and attractive physiques, yet some (believers) are also blessed with spiritual blessings in accordance to Ephesians 1:3 NKJV *"Blessed be the God and Father of our Lord Jesus Christ, who hath blessed us with all spiritual blessings in heavenly places in Christ."*

Anytime you notice a blessing of God in your life, God is reminding you of His expectation to have fruits. Fruits are God's return on investment over your life. The blessing is God's gift to you, but the fruits you bear with it are your offerings to God. This illustrates the cycle of divine purpose. To be unfruitful is to alter this divine cycle and the consequences are regrets. Fruitfulness is not for us to negotiate with God; rather, it is His divine mandate ordained for our benefit.

At a breakfast meeting, a pastor friend of mine once shared the story of two discouraged missionaries to Asia who felt that their ten years on the mission field were not fruitful enough. We were shocked to hear that their heeding God's call and serving Him faithfully away from their home country could end in discouragement. Sometimes, what we define by our understanding as fruits may be mere leaves to God.

We must not be ignorant of Satan's effort to twist the word of God with regards to foretold events, but God had assured us that His words will accomplish His determined purpose (see Isaiah 55:11 NKJV). We also read in Hebrews 4:12 NKJV that God's word is life-giving and powerful; always produce fruits. Hence, our job is to simply plant the word of God wherever we find ourselves and leave the results to Him. His ways are not our ways.

Jonah, the Prophet, became fruitful in his calling when he delivered God's word to the people of Nineveh the entire nation including their animals repented! Yes, despite Jonah's success, he was so discouraged that he wanted to commit suicide. His protest to God was aptly captured in Jonah 4:3 NKJV where he cried out, *"Therefore now, O Lord, please take my life from me, for it is better for me to die than to live!"*

God expects his children to be fruitful because of His blessing on them, but some Christians have limited fruitfulness to biological reproduction. So, when their marriage lacks the fruit of the womb, they conclude that they're also unfruitful in other areas of their life. On the other hand, when some have children, they assumed they're already fruitful and thus cease striving for success in other areas of their lives. God desires for us to deploy our creativity, our intellect, our physical gifts for His Kingdom's service and the fruits of our lips to declare His glory. If you're a gifted singer, sing His praises and if you're gifted with strength, use it to labour in His vineyard.

A fruitless man owes God a debt he can never repay in his lifetime. Therefore, there's no tenable reason for any man to be fruitless because we were all blessed in Adam by God's command to be fruitful. Even plants bear fruits as proof of God's blessings. One of the proofs of our spiritual maturity is our ability to bear fruits that abide. Here are three truths that attest to our fruitfulness as decreed by God, the Father:

The first is that God delights in the resurrection of the dead. God always intervenes when things that ought to live die and raise them up to His glory. Therefore, it is not too late for you to bear fruits. You see, despite the deadness of Abraham and Sarah's reproductive systems, they were still able to birth Isaac, the child of promise.

Secondly, the weaker we are, the stronger God is. God is always drawn to the weak because His power is fully expressed in our weaknesses hence, we should rejoice even in our weaknesses (see 2 Corinthians 12:9 NKJV).

Thirdly, when God prunes you, He is preparing you for greater fruits. Therefore, when things go wrong or we are in pain, we should choose to be excited and wait for God to come through for us. Remind yourself daily that, "I am made to grow, flourish, blossom and produce fruits, and nothing can stop my fruitfulness."

PROGRESS SHOTS:

1. Father, please help me to produce fruits as expected; spiritually, physically, emotionally and biologically.
2. Lord, make my feet like a hind's feet and set me on my high places.
3. I will grow up, blossom, be fruitful and excel in Jesus' name.

FROM STAGNATION TO PROGRESS

TEXT: DEUTERONOMY 1:6 NKJV

"The Lord our God spoke to us in Horeb, saying: 'You have dwelt long enough at this mountain...'"

KEY NUGGET: **You are created with the ability to keep growing and developing. Discover your inborn strength and believe in your God.**

Inertia is defined as a state of idleness (or passivity) hence, an object in a state of inertia will stay so until it is acted upon by an external force greater than the one that puts it to rest. It is natural for man to resist change until moved upon through persuasion, inspiration or coercion. There is a limit to which a man can progress in his effort; a divine force must be applied to his heart to advance before advancing further.

In today's text, the strongest force that altered Israel's inertia was the Word of God. So, to advance into God's promises, we must keep hearing God's Word. A man who fails to hear God will remain spiritually static in life. Our God is a God of perfect timing and would always take us deeper into His promises until our final breath.

Progress is designed to prevent us from settling in our comfort zone and steers us into uncharted territories. Ask yourself where have you dwelt for too long? Many people have dwelt too long in excuses, complaints, delusions, mediocrity, etc., and even pitched their tents there before they could reach their excellent best. The mountain God commanded the Israelites to move away from was a place of temporary comfort and provision, but they almost turned it into a permanent abode. Sometimes, people refrain midway on the road to their destiny because of a temporary support they encountered, thereby abandoning the Promised Land.

Some people reside in the land of strategy and analysis until they die of spiritual paralysis. They have all the plans and patterns written on paper but are too afraid to take the necessary steps in translating their dreams into reality. Some potential businesses are relying on solely paid salary at the detriment of the multinational visions God has lined up for them. Some ministers are confined to religious activities and under the roof of tradition when they ought to launch their nets into deeper waters of exploits for the Lord. Stagnation is defined as remaining in one spot for an unnecessarily long time; it is like staying the same without growing or changing.

Stagnant people can be held captive by a stronger power than theirs, by the devil, or by their own thoughts. Stagnation breeds an average and unfulfilled life, but success in life is a function of accumulated progress. You cannot remain where you used to be and expect to become who you ought to be.

The story of the man at the pool of Bethesda who was plagued with an infirmity for thirty-eight years is a good illustration of stagnation. The enemy has robbed this man of his prime years. In some cultures, a child born within this period could be a grandfather, even at thirty-eight! Jesus knew this impotent man had been stagnant for a while so the first thing He offered the man was a choice to be made well. In John 5:6 NKJV we read, *"When Jesus saw him lying there, and knew that he already had been in that condition a long time, He said to him, 'Do you want to be made well?'"*

The man was lying there as if he had found rest in his dysfunctional state. There seems to be a tendency for sick people to find comfort and identity in the company of other sick people because they have something in common. Hence, a man can be so infirmed that he no longer expects to be healed but wishes that everyone around him stays sick.

The posture of our man at the pool of Bethesda is another indication that, apart from him having a poor health condition, he had also been in that condition for a long time. Jesus did not assume that the man wanted to be healed so He had to ask first. So, I also ask you, "Do you want to be healed from the infirmity of excuses, procrastination and the blame game?" The next phase of your encounter with God may depend on your response to that.

Stagnation can be caused by such things as pride, ignorance, errors, etc., but for the man at the pool of Bethesda, it was sin. Many people have become lawful captives of pornography, drugs, bitterness, fear, pessimism, etc. (See Isaiah 49:24-26 NKJV.)

You can overcome stagnation by embracing the truth of the Word of God. You need to examine yourself, find out where you have erred and make the necessary corrections. Strive to develop an acquired taste for God's word, obey His instructions, and trust Him to fulfill His promises in your life. Jesus later told the impotent man in John 5:14 NKJV, "*See, you have been made well. Sin no more, lest a worse thing come upon you.*" God is interested in your progress so, be assured of the path He has marked out for your progress with the following passages of scriptures:

"But the path of the just is as the shining light, that shines more and more unto the perfect day" (Proverbs 4:18 KJV).

"They go from strength to strength, every one of them in Zion appears before God" (Psalms 84:7 KJV).

PRAYER SHOTS:

1. Father, please teach my fingers to fight and my hands to war.
2. Lord, please set my life and my destiny in the right motion.
3. My mouth is bigger than my mountains; I, therefore, declare that I receive unimpeded progress in Jesus' name.

DAY

31

YOU CAN EVEN BEAT THE ODDS

TEXT: LUKE 1:37 NKJV

"For with God nothing will be impossible."

Key Nugget: **Don't get distracted when life brings challenging situations your way; focus on the finishing line and believe that you can push through any obstacle with God on your side.**

Challenges seem impossible to overcome when God is not in the picture. Our text does deny that we face impossible situations as humans, but it however assures us that all things are possible when we entrust them to God. Many people sow seeds, plan meetings to curry favour of celebrities and prophets so they can achieve certain feats in life. Despite their best efforts, certain areas of their lives are still dominated by impossibilities. People capture moments in photos, post selfies and hang pictures on their walls to keep appearances, but their lives are still overwhelmed with impossibilities.

All things are possible with God. The giants and hindrances we face that seem insurmountable are there until we partner with God in dealing with them. Working with God does mean we become idle and leave Him with our responsibilities. Rather, we trust Him for guidance in implementing strategies and principles (as instructed by the Holy Spirit) to deal with our problems.

We must learn to be on the same page with God by aligning with His will and being obedient to His Word. We can't be working in contradiction to God and expect our mountains to move. We must strive to be in a consistent fellowship with God. Because of the many things canvassing for the believer's attention in our time, people join associations and groups to garner their support when trouble comes, but such a move doesn't guarantee victory. When we're truly linked with God in spirit and in truth, things that look initially impossible will eventually turn into testimonies.

"AND AS THOSE WHO BORE THE ARK CAME TO THE JORDAN, AND THE FEET OF THE PRIESTS WHO BORE THE ARK DIPPED IN THE EDGE OF THE WATER (FOR THE JORDAN OVERFLOWS ALL ITS BANKS DURING THE WHOLE TIME OF HARVEST), THAT THE WATERS WHICH CAME DOWN FROM UPSTREAM STOOD STILL, AND ROSE IN A HEAP VERY FAR AWAY AT ADAM, THE CITY THAT IS BESIDE ZARETAN. SO THE WATERS THAT WENT DOWN INTO THE SEA OF THE ARABAH, THE SALT SEA, FAILED, AND WERE CUT OFF; AND THE PEOPLE CROSSED OVER OPPOSITE JERICHO" (JOSHUA 3:15-16 NKJV).

Even though Jordan overflowed its banks, when the feet of the men carrying the ark touched its shores, the river stood still, rose in a heap and went in another direction so God's covenant nation of God. The water was cut off from its usual course so the people can cross to the other side of Jericho! No gimmicks, no civil engineering ingenuity, no gulf and drainages; only the presence of God symbolized by the ark, was enough to make the massive water flow find a new course. My prayer for you is that as you carry God's presence, whatever represents an overflow of water in your body or your marriage that is hindering you from crossing over to God's purposes for your life will surely be cut off.

When you yield yourself to God as His sanctuary and make your heart His domain, then you will experience Israel's kind of testimony in Psalm 114:3-4 KJV: *"The sea saw it, and fled: Jordan was driven back. The mountains skipped like rams, and the little hills like lambs."*

They don't flee because of you, because of God's presence with you! When God is involved in your dealings you will stop running from things that should be running from you.

In my family's early years in South Africa, our second child (a baby girl) was born. We were excited at having a girl because our first child was a boy and so, my wife and I concluded that our family is now complete. We, therefore, decided to celebrate the new addition to the family by inviting friends and colleagues from all over South Africa who came dressed in their elegant attires and luxury cars. Our home at that time was inside a gated community located in a very conservative part of the city, and we were the only black family there.

Some of our neighbours have never witnessed a large gathering of black people with such display opulence before. You can imagine then why the sudden influx of so many black people in their regal attire and luxury cars into our community did not sit well with our neighbors.

In reaction to this, a disgruntled neighbour decided to block one of our guests' vehicles with his own. So, we pleaded with him to remove his car when it was time for my guest to leave, but he refused. Instead, this man started swearing at us. Somebody suggested that the only way out was to lift the man's car out of the way. Still dressed our elegant attires, we all lifted the car out of the way for my friend to drive out. We all shouted for joy and celebrated our amazing feat to the chagrin of my angry neighbour.

That day, I learnt a very valuable lesson: you can remove any obstacles and eliminate barriers standing in your way. No matter how huge or impossible it may look, barriers can give way, walls can be moved, barricades can be destroyed, gates can be lifted, chains can be broken, and inhibitions can yield.

PRAYER SHOTS:

1. Father please increase my faith to believe you and break free from all forms of limitations.
2. Lord, please remove strains, stress, and suffering from my life in Jesus' name.
3. I declare that I am entering a new realm of possibilities in Jesus' name.

Printed in the United States
By Bookmasters